HOMO SACER

M E R I D I A N

Crossing Aesthetics

Werner Hamacher
& David E. Wellbery
Editors

Translated by
Daniel Heller-Roazen

*Stanford
University
Press*

*Stanford
California*

HOMO SACER

*Sovereign Power
and Bare Life*

Giorgio Agamben

Homo Sacer: Sovereign Power and Bare Life
was originally published as *Homo sacer: Il potere sovrano e la
nuda vita,* © 1995 Giulio Einaudi editore s.p.a.

Stanford University Press
Stanford, California

© 1998 by the Board of Trustees of the
Leland Stanford Junior University

Printed in the United States of America

CIP data appear at the end of the book

Contents

Das Recht hat kein Dasein für sich, sein Wesen vielmehr ist das Leben der Menschen selbst, von einer Seite angesehen.

—Savigny

Law has no existence for itself; rather its essence lies, from a certain perspective, in the very life of men.

Ita in iure civitatis, civiumque officiis investigandis opus est, non quidem ut dissolvatur civitas, sed tamen ut tanquam dissoluta consideretur, id est, ut qualis sit natura humana, quibus rebus ad civitatem compaginandam apta vel inepta sit, et quomodo homines inter se componi debeant, qui coalescere volunt, recte intelligatur.

—Hobbes

To make a more curious search into the rights of States, and duties of Subjects, it is necessary, (I say not to take them in sunder, but yet that) they be so considered, as if they were dissolved, (i.e.) that wee rightly understand what the quality of humane nature is, in what matters it is, in what not fit to make up a civill government, and how men must be agreed among themselves, that intend to grow up into a well-grounded State.

Euretē moi hē entolē hē eis zōēn, autē eis thanaton.

—Saint Paul

And the commandment, which was ordained to life, I found to be unto death.

HOMO SACER

*Sovereign Power
and Bare Life*

Introduction

The Greeks had no single term to express what we mean by the word "life." They used two terms that, although traceable to a common etymological root, are semantically and morphologically distinct: *zoē*, which expressed the simple fact of living common to all living beings (animals, men, or gods), and *bios*, which indicated the form or way of living proper to an individual or a group. When Plato mentions three kinds of life in the *Philebus*, and when Aristotle distinguishes the contemplative life of the philosopher (*bios theōrētikos*) from the life of pleasure (*bios apolaustikos*) and the political life (*bios politikos*) in the *Nichomachean Ethics*, neither philosopher would ever have used the term *zoē* (which in Greek, significantly enough, lacks a plural). This follows from the simple fact that what was at issue for both thinkers was not at all simple natural life but rather a qualified life, a particular way of life. Concerning God, Aristotle can certainly speak of a *zoē aristē kai aidios*, a more noble and eternal life (*Metaphysics*, 1072b, 28), but only insofar as he means to underline the significant truth that even God is a living being (similarly, Aristotle uses the term *zoē* in the same context—and in a way that is just as meaningful—to define the act of thinking). But to speak of a *zoē politikē* of the citizens of Athens would have made no sense. Not that the classical world had no familiarity with the idea that natural life, simple *zoē* as such, could be a good in itself. In a passage of the *Politics*, after noting that the end of the city is life according to the good, Aristotle expresses his awareness of that idea with the most perfect lucidity:

> This [life according to the good] is the greatest end both in common for all men and for each man separately. But men also come together and maintain the political community in view of simple living, because there is probably some kind of good in the mere fact of living itself [*kata to zēn auto monon*]. If there is no great difficulty as to the way of life [*kata ton bion*], clearly most men will tolerate much suffering and hold on to life [*zoē*] as if it were a kind of serenity [*euēmeria*, beautiful day] and a natural sweetness. (1278b, 23–31)

In the classical world, however, simple natural life is excluded from the *polis* in the strict sense, and remains confined—as merely reproductive life—to the sphere of the *oikos*, "home" (*Politics*, 1252a, 26–35). At the beginning of the *Politics*, Aristotle takes the greatest care to distinguish the *oikonomos* (the head of an estate) and the *despotēs* (the head of the family), both of whom are concerned with the reproduction and the subsistence of life, from the politician, and he scorns those who think the difference between the two is one of quantity and not of kind. And when Aristotle defined the end of the perfect community in a passage that was to become canonical for the political tradition of the West (1252b, 30), he did so precisely by opposing the simple fact of living (*to zēn*) to politically qualified life (*to eu zēn*): *ginomenē men oun tou zēn heneken, ousa de tou eu zēn*, "born with regard to life, but existing essentially with regard to the good life" (in the Latin translation of William of Moerbeke, which both Aquinas and Marsilius of Padua had before them: *facta quidem igitur vivendi gratia, existens autem gratia bene vivendi*).

It is true that in a famous passage of the same work, Aristotle defines man as a *politikon zōon* (*Politics*, 1253a, 4). But here (aside from the fact that in Attic Greek the verb *bionai* is practically never used in the present tense), "political" is not an attribute of the living being as such, but rather a specific difference that determines the genus *zōon*. (Only a little later, after all, human politics is distinguished from that of other living beings in that it is founded, through a supplement of politicity [*policità*] tied to language, on a community not simply of the pleasant and the painful but of the good and the evil and of the just and the unjust.)

Michel Foucault refers to this very definition when, at the end of the first volume of *The History of Sexuality*, he summarizes the process by which, at the threshold of the modern era, natural life begins to be included in the mechanisms and calculations of State power, and politics turns into *biopolitics*. "For millennia," he writes, "man remained what he was for Aristotle: a living animal with the additional capacity for political existence; modern man is an animal whose politics calls his existence as a living being into question" (*La volonté*, p. 188).

According to Foucault, a society's "threshold of biological modernity" is situated at the point at which the species and the individual as a simple living body become what is at stake in a society's political strategies. After 1977, the courses at the Collège de France start to focus on the passage from the "territorial State" to the "State of population" and on the resulting increase in importance of the nation's health and biological life as a problem of sovereign power, which is then gradually transformed into a "government of men" (*Dits et écrits*, 3: 719). "What follows is a kind of bestialization of man achieved through the most sophisticated political techniques. For the first time in history, the possibilities of the social sciences are made known, and at once it becomes possible both to protect life and to authorize a holocaust." In particular, the development and triumph of capitalism would not have been possible, from this perspective, without the disciplinary control achieved by the new bio-power, which, through a series of appropriate technologies, so to speak created the "docile bodies" that it needed.

Almost twenty years before *The History of Sexuality*, Hannah Arendt had already analyzed the process that brings *homo laborans*—and, with it, biological life as such—gradually to occupy the very center of the political scene of modernity. In *The Human Condition*, Arendt attributes the transformation and decadence of the political realm in modern societies to this very primacy of natural life over political action. That Foucault was able to begin his study of biopolitics with no reference to Arendt's work (which remains, even today, practically without continuation) bears witness to the difficulties and resistances that thinking had to encounter in this area. And it is most likely these very difficulties that account for the curious fact that Arendt establishes no connection between her research in *The Human Condition* and the penetrating analyses she had previously devoted to totalitarian power (in which a biopolitical perspective is altogether lacking), and that Foucault, in just as striking a fashion, never dwelt on the exemplary places of modern biopolitics: the concentration camp and the structure of the great totalitarian states of the twentieth century.

Foucault's death kept him from showing how he would have developed the concept and study of biopolitics. In any case, however, the entry of *zoē* into the sphere of the *polis*—the politicization of bare life as such—constitutes the decisive event of modernity and signals a radical transformation of the political-philosophical categories of classical thought. It is even likely that if politics today seems to be passing through a lasting eclipse, this is because politics has failed to reckon with this foundational event of modernity. The "enigmas" (Furet, *L'Allemagne nazi*, p. 7) that our century has proposed to historical reason and that remain with us (Nazism is only the most disquieting among them) will be solved only on the terrain—biopolitics—on which they were formed. Only within a biopolitical horizon will it be possible to decide whether the categories whose opposition founded modern politics (right/left, private/public, absolutism/democracy, etc.)—and which have been steadily dissolving, to the point of entering today into a real zone of indistinction—will have to be abandoned or will, instead, eventually regain the meaning they lost in that very horizon. And only a reflection that, taking up Foucault's and Benjamin's suggestion, thematically interrogates the link between bare life and politics, a link that secretly governs the modern ideologies seemingly most distant from one another, will be able to bring the political out of its concealment and, at the same time, return thought to its practical calling.

One of the most persistent features of Foucault's work is its decisive abandonment of the traditional approach to the problem of power, which is based on juridico-institutional models (the definition of sovereignty, the theory of the State), in favor of an unprejudiced analysis of the concrete ways in which power penetrates subjects' very bodies and forms of life. As shown by a seminar held in 1982 at the University of Vermont, in his final years Foucault seemed to orient this analysis according to two distinct directives for research: on the one hand, the study of the *political techniques* (such as the science of the police) with which the State assumes and integrates the care of the natural life of individuals into its very center; on the other hand, the examination of the *technologies of the self* by which processes of subjectivization bring the individual to bind himself to his own identity and consciousness and, at the same time, to an external power. Clearly these two lines (which carry on two tendencies present in Foucault's work from the very beginning) intersect in many points and refer back to a common center. In one of his last writings, Foucault argues that the modern Western state has integrated techniques of subjective individualization with procedures of objective totalization to an unprecedented degree, and he speaks of a real "political 'double bind,' constituted by individualization and the simultaneous totalization of structures of modern power" (*Dits et écrits*, 4: 229–32).

Yet the point at which these two faces of power converge remains strangely unclear in Foucault's work, so much so that it has even been claimed that Foucault would have consistently refused to elaborate a unitary theory of power. If Foucault contests the traditional approach to the problem of power, which is exclusively based on juridical models ("What legitimates power?") or on institutional models ("What is the State?"), and if he calls for a "liberation from the theoretical privilege of sovereignty" in order to construct an analytic of power that would not take law as its model and code, then where, in the body of power, is the zone of indistinction (or, at least, the point of intersection) at which techniques of individualization and totalizing procedures converge? And, more generally, is there a unitary center in which the political "double bind" finds its *raison d'être*? That there is a subjective aspect in the genesis of power was already implicit in the concept of *servitude volontaire* in Étienne de La Boétie. But what is the point at which the voluntary servitude of individuals comes into contact with objective power? Can one be content, in such a delicate area, with psychological explanations such as the suggestive notion of a parallelism between external and internal neuroses? Confronted with phenomena such as the power of the society of the spectacle that is everywhere transforming the political realm today, is it legitimate or even possible to hold subjective technologies and political techniques apart?

Although the existence of such a line of thinking seems to be logically implicit in Foucault's work, it remains a blind spot to the eye of the researcher, or rather something like a vanishing point that the different perspectival lines of Foucault's inquiry (and, more generally, of the entire Western reflection on power) converge toward without reaching.

The present inquiry concerns precisely this hidden point of intersection between the juridico-institutional and the biopolitical models of power. What this work has had to record among its likely conclusions is precisely that the two analyses cannot be separated, and that the inclusion of bare life in the political realm constitutes the original—if concealed—nucleus of sovereign power. *It can even be said that the production of a biopolitical body is the original activity of sovereign power.* In this sense, biopolitics is at least as old as the sovereign exception. Placing biological life at the center of its calculations, the modern State therefore does nothing other than bring to light the secret tie uniting power and bare life, thereby reaffirming the bond (derived from a tenacious correspondence between the modern and the archaic which one encounters in the most diverse spheres) between modern power and the most immemorial of the *arcana imperii*.

If this is true, it will be necessary to reconsider the sense of the Aristotelian definition of the *polis* as the opposition between life (*zēn*) and good life (*eu zēn*). The opposition is, in fact, at the same time an implication of the first in the second, of bare life in politically qualified life. What remains to be interrogated in the Aristotelian definition is not merely—as has been assumed until now—the sense, the modes, and the possible articulations of the "good life" as the *telos* of the political. We must instead ask why Western politics first constitutes itself through an exclusion (which is simultaneously an inclusion) of bare life. What is the relation between politics and life, if life presents itself as what is included by means of an exclusion?

The structure of the exception delineated in the first part of this book appears from this perspective to be consubstantial with Western politics. In Foucault's statement according to which man was, for Aristotle, a "living animal with the additional capacity for political existence," it is therefore precisely the meaning of this "additional capacity" that must be understood as problematic. The peculiar phrase "born with regard to life, but existing essentially with regard to the good life" can be read not only as an implication of being born (*ginomenē*) in being (*ousa*), but also as an inclusive exclusion (an *exceptio*) of *zoē* in the *polis*, almost as if politics were the place in which life had to transform itself into good life and in which what had to be politicized were always already bare life. In Western politics, bare life has the peculiar privilege of being that whose exclusion founds the city of men.

It is not by chance, then, that a passage of the *Politics* situates the proper place of the *polis* in the transition from voice to language. The link between bare life and politics is the same link that the metaphysical definition of man as "the living being who has language" seeks in the relation between *phonē* and *logos*:

> Among living beings, only man has language. The voice is the sign of pain and pleasure, and this is why it belongs to other living beings (since their nature has developed to the point of having the sensations of pain and pleasure and of signifying the two). But language is for

manifesting the fitting and the unfitting and the just and the unjust. To
have the sensation of the good and the bad and of the just and the unjust is what is proper to men as opposed to other living beings, and the
community of these things makes dwelling and the city. (1253a, 10–18)

The question "In what way does the living being have language?" corresponds exactly to the question "In what way does bare
life dwell in the *polis?*" The living being has *logos* by taking away
and conserving its own voice in it, even as it dwells in the *polis* by
letting its own bare life be excluded, as an exception, within it.
Politics therefore appears as the truly fundamental structure of
Western metaphysics insofar as it occupies the threshold on which
the relation between the living being and the *logos* is realized. In the
"politicization" of bare life—the metaphysical task *par excellence*—
the humanity of living man is decided. In assuming this task,
modernity does nothing other than declare its own faithfulness to
the essential structure of the metaphysical tradition. The fundamental categorial pair of Western politics is not that of friend/
enemy but that of bare life/political existence, *zoē/bios*, exclu-
sion/inclusion. There is politics because man is the living being
who, in language, separates and opposes himself to his own bare
life and, at the same time, maintains himself in relation to that bare
life in an inclusive exclusion.

The protagonist of this book is bare life, that is, the life of *homo
sacer* (sacred man), who *may be killed and yet not sacrificed*, and
whose essential function in modern politics we intend to assert. An
obscure figure of archaic Roman law, in which human life is
included in the juridical order [*ordinamento*]¹ solely in the form of
its exclusion (that is, of its capacity to be killed), has thus offered
the key by which not only the sacred texts of sovereignty but also
the very codes of political power will unveil their mysteries. At the

1. "Order" renders the Italian *ordinamento*, which carries the sense not only of
order but of political and juridical rule, regulation, and system. The word
ordinamento is also the Italian translation of Carl Schmitt's *Ordnung*. Where the
author refers to *ordinamento* as *Ordnung*, the English word used is the one chosen
by Schmitt's translators, "ordering."—Trans.

same time, however, this ancient meaning of the term *sacer* presents us with the enigma of a figure of the sacred that, before or beyond the religious, constitutes the first paradigm of the political realm of the West. The Foucauldian thesis will then have to be corrected or, at least, completed, in the sense that what characterizes modern politics is not so much the inclusion of *zoē* in the *polis*—which is, in itself, absolutely ancient—nor simply the fact that life as such becomes a principal object of the projections and calculations of State power. Instead the decisive fact is that, together with the process by which the exception everywhere becomes the rule, the realm of bare life—which is originally situated at the margins of the political order—gradually begins to coincide with the political realm, and exclusion and inclusion, outside and inside, *bios* and *zoē*, right and fact, enter into a zone of irreducible indistinction. At once excluding bare life from and capturing it within the political order, the state of exception actually constituted, in its very separateness, the hidden foundation on which the entire political system rested. When its borders begin to be blurred, the bare life that dwelt there frees itself in the city and becomes both subject and object of the conflicts of the political order, the one place for both the organization of State power and emancipation from it. Everything happens as if, along with the disciplinary process by which State power makes man as a living being into its own specific object, another process is set in motion that in large measure corresponds to the birth of modern democracy, in which man as a living being presents himself no longer as an *object* but as the *subject* of political power. These processes—which in many ways oppose and (at least apparently) bitterly conflict with each other—nevertheless converge insofar as both concern the bare life of the citizen, the new biopolitical body of humanity.

If anything characterizes modern democracy as opposed to classical democracy, then, it is that modern democracy presents itself from the beginning as a vindication and liberation of *zoē*, and that it is constantly trying to transform its own bare life into a way of life and to find, so to speak, the *bios* of *zoē*. Hence, too, modern democracy's specific aporia: it wants to put the freedom and happi-

ness of men into play in the very place—"bare life"—that marked
their subjection. Behind the long, strife-ridden process that leads to
the recognition of rights and formal liberties stands once again the
body of the sacred man with his double sovereign, his life that
cannot be sacrificed yet may, nevertheless, be killed. To become
conscious of this aporia is not to belittle the conquests and accom-
plishments of democracy. It is, rather, to try to understand once
and for all why democracy, at the very moment in which it seemed
to have finally triumphed over its adversaries and reached its
greatest height, proved itself incapable of saving *zoē*, to whose
happiness it had dedicated all its efforts, from unprecedented ruin.
Modern democracy's decadence and gradual convergence with
totalitarian states in post-democratic spectacular societies (which
begins to become evident with Alexis de Tocqueville and finds its
final sanction in the analyses of Guy Debord) may well be rooted in
this aporia, which marks the beginning of modern democracy and
forces it into complicity with its most implacable enemy. Today
politics knows no value (and, consequently, no nonvalue) other
than life, and until the contradictions that this fact implies are
dissolved, Nazism and fascism—which transformed the decision
on bare life into the supreme political principle—will remain stub-
bornly with us. According to the testimony of Robert Antelme, in
fact, what the camps taught those who lived there was precisely that
"calling into question the quality of man provokes an almost
biological assertion of belonging to the human race" (*L'éspèce humaine*, p. 11).

The idea of an inner solidarity between democracy and totalitarianism (which here we must, with every caution, advance) is
obviously not (like Leo Strauss's thesis concerning the secret convergence of the final goals of liberalism and communism) a historiographical claim, which would authorize the liquidation and
leveling of the enormous differences that characterize their history
and their rivalry. Yet this idea must nevertheless be strongly maintained on a historico-philosophical level, since it alone will allow us
to orient ourselves in relation to the new realities and unforeseen
convergences of the end of the millennium. This idea alone will

make it possible to clear the way for the new politics, which remains largely to be invented.

In contrasting the "beautiful day" (*euēmeria*) of simple life with the "great difficulty" of political *bios* in the passage cited above, Aristotle may well have given the most beautiful formulation to the aporia that lies at the foundation of Western politics. The 24 centuries that have since gone by have brought only provisional and ineffective solutions. In carrying out the metaphysical task that has led it more and more to assume the form of a biopolitics, Western politics has not succeeded in constructing the link between *zoē* and *bios*, between voice and language, that would have healed the fracture. Bare life remains included in politics in the form of the exception, that is, as something that is included solely through an exclusion. How is it possible to "politicize" the "natural sweetness" of *zoē*? And first of all, does *zoē* really need to be politicized, or is politics not already contained in *zoē* as its most precious center? The biopolitics of both modern totalitarianism and the society of mass hedonism and consumerism certainly constitute answers to these questions. Nevertheless, until a completely new politics—that is, a politics no longer founded on the *exceptio* of bare life—is at hand, every theory and every praxis will remain imprisoned and immobile, and the "beautiful day" of life will be given citizenship only either through blood and death or in the perfect senselessness to which the society of the spectacle condemns it.

Carl Schmitt's definition of sovereignty ("Sovereign is he who decides on the state of exception") became a commonplace even before there was any understanding that what was at issue in it was nothing less than the limit concept of the doctrine of law and the State, in which sovereignty borders (since every limit concept is always the limit between two concepts) on the sphere of life and becomes indistinguishable from it. As long as the form of the State constituted the fundamental horizon of all communal life and the political, religious, juridical, and economic doctrines that sustained this form were still strong, this "most extreme sphere" could not truly come to light. The problem of sovereignty was reduced to the question of who within the political order was invested with certain powers, and the very threshold of the political order itself was never called into question. Today, now that the great State structures have entered into a process of dissolution and the emergency has, as Walter Benjamin foresaw, become the rule, the time is ripe to place the problem of the originary structure and limits of the form of the State in a new perspective. The weakness of anarchist and Marxian critiques of the State was precisely to have not caught sight of this structure and thus to have quickly left the *arcanum imperii* aside, as if it had no substance outside of the simulacra and the ideologies invoked to justify it. But one ends up identifying with an enemy whose structure one does not understand, and the theory of the State (and in particular of the state of exception, which is to say, of the dictatorship of the proletariat as the transitional phase leading to the stateless society) is the reef on which the revolutions of our century have been shipwrecked.

This book, which was originally conceived as a response to the bloody mystification of a new planetary order, therefore had to reckon with problems—first of all that of the sacredness of life— which the author had not, in the beginning, foreseen. In the course of the undertaking, however, it became clear that one cannot, in such an area, accept as a guarantee any of the notions that the social sciences (from jurisprudence to anthropology) thought they had defined or presupposed as evident, and that many of these notions demanded—in the urgency of catastrophe—to be revised without reserve.

PART ONE

The Logic of Sovereignty

§ 1 The Paradox of Sovereignty

1.1. The paradox of sovereignty consists in the fact the sovereign is, at the same time, outside and inside the juridical order. If the sovereign is truly the one to whom the juridical order grants the power of proclaiming a state of exception and, therefore, of suspending the order's own validity, then "the sovereign stands outside the juridical order and, nevertheless, belongs to it, since it is up to him to decide if the constitution is to be suspended *in toto*" (Schmitt, *Politische Theologie*, p. 13). The specification that the sovereign is "*at the same time* outside and inside the juridical order" (emphasis added) is not insignificant: the sovereign, having the legal power to suspend the validity of the law, legally places himself outside the law. This means that the paradox can also be formulated this way: "the law is outside itself," or: "I, the sovereign, who am outside the law, declare that there is nothing outside the law [*che non c'è un fuori legge*]."

The topology implicit in the paradox is worth reflecting upon, since the degree to which sovereignty marks the limit (in the double sense of end and principle) of the juridical order will become clear only once the structure of the paradox is grasped. Schmitt presents this structure as the structure of the exception (*Ausnahme*):

The exception is that which cannot be subsumed; it defies general codification, but it simultaneously reveals a specifically juridical for-

mal element: the decision in absolute purity. The exception appears in
its absolute form when it is a question of creating a situation in which
juridical rules can be valid. Every general rule demands a regular,
everyday frame of life to which it can be factually applied and which is
submitted to its regulations. The rule requires a homogeneous medium. This factual regularity is not merely an "external presupposition" that the jurist can ignore; it belongs, rather, to the rule's imma-
nent validity. There is no rule that is applicable to chaos. Order must
be established for juridical order to make sense. A regular situation
must be created, and sovereign is he who definitely decides if this
situation is actually effective. All law is "situational law." The sovereign
creates and guarantees the situation as a whole in its totality. He has
the monopoly over the final decision. Therein consists the essence of
State sovereignty, which must therefore be properly juridically defined
not as the monopoly to sanction or to rule but as the monopoly to
decide, where the word "monopoly" is used in a general sense that is
still to be developed. The decision reveals the essence of State authority most clearly. Here the decision must be distinguished from the
juridical regulation, and (to formulate it paradoxically) authority
proves itself not to need law to create law. . . . The exception is more
interesting than the regular case. The latter proves nothing; the exception proves everything. The exception does not only confirm the rule;
the rule as such lives off the exception alone. A Protestant theologian
who demonstrated the vital intensity of which theological reflection
was still capable in the nineteenth century said: "The exception
explains the general and itself. And when one really wants to study the
general, one need only look around for a real exception. It brings
everything to light more clearly than the general itself. After a while,
one becomes disgusted with the endless talk about the general—there
are exceptions. If they cannot be explained, then neither can the
general be explained. Usually the difficulty is not noticed, since the
general is thought about not with passion but only with comfortable
superficiality. The exception, on the other hand, thinks the general
with intense passion." (*Politische Theologie*, pp. 19–22)

It is not by chance that in defining the exception Schmitt refers
to the work of a theologian (who is none other than Søren Kierke-
gaard). Giambattista Vico had, to be sure, affirmed the superiority

of the exception, which he called "the ultimate configuration of facts," over positive law in a way which was not so dissimilar: "An esteemed jurist is, therefore, not someone who, with the help of a good memory, masters positive law [or the general complex of laws], but rather someone who, with sharp judgment, knows how to look into cases and see the ultimate circumstances of facts that merit equitable consideration and exceptions from general rules" (*De antiquissima*, chap. 2). Yet nowhere in the realm of the juridical sciences can one find a theory that grants such a high position to the exception. For what is at issue in the sovereign exception is, according to Schmitt, the very condition of possibility of juridical rule and, along with it, the very meaning of State authority. Through the state of exception, the sovereign "creates and guarantees the situation" that the law needs for its own validity. But what is this "situation," what is its structure, such that it consists in nothing other than the suspension of the rule?

ℵ The Vichian opposition between positive law (*ius theticum*) and exception well expresses the particular status of the exception. The exception is an element in law that transcends positive law in the form of its suspension. The exception is to positive law what negative theology is to positive theology. While the latter affirms and predicates determinate qualities of God, negative (or mystical) theology, with its "neither ... nor ... ," negates and suspends the attribution to God of any predicate whatsoever. Yet negative theology is not outside theology and can actually be shown to function as the principle grounding the possibility in general of anything like a theology. Only because it has been negatively presupposed as what subsists outside any possible predicate can divinity become the subject of a predication. Analogously, only because its validity is suspended in the state of exception can positive law define the normal case as the realm of its own validity.

1.2. The exception is a kind of exclusion. What is excluded from the general rule is an individual case. But the most proper characteristic of the exception is that what is excluded in it is not, on account of being excluded, absolutely without relation to the rule. On the contrary, what is excluded in the exception maintains itself in relation to the rule in the form of the rule's suspension. *The rule applies to the exception in no longer applying, in withdrawing from it.* The state of exception is thus not the chaos that precedes order but rather the situation that results from its suspension. In this sense, the exception is truly, according to its etymological root, *taken outside* (*ex-capere*), and not simply excluded.

It has often been observed that the juridico-political order has the structure of an inclusion of what is simultaneously pushed outside. Gilles Deleuze and Félix Guattari were thus able to write, "Sovereignty only rules over what it is capable of interiorizing" (Deleuze and Guattari, *Mille plateaux*, p. 445); and, concerning the "great confinement" described by Foucault in his *Madness and Civilization*, Maurice Blanchot spoke of society's attempt to "confine the outside" (*enfermer le dehors*), that is, to constitute it in an "interiority of expectation or of exception." Confronted with an excess, the system interiorizes what exceeds it through an interdiction and in this way "designates itself as exterior to itself" (*L'entretien infini*, p. 292). The exception that defines the structure of sovereignty is, however, even more complex. Here what is outside is included not simply by means of an interdiction or an internment, but rather by means of the suspension of the juridical order's validity—by letting the juridical order, that is, withdraw from the exception and abandon it. The exception does not subtract itself from the rule; rather, the rule, suspending itself, gives rise to the exception and, maintaining itself in relation to the exception, first constitutes itself as a rule. The particular "force" of law consists in this capacity of law to maintain itself in relation to an exteriority. We shall give the name *relation of exception* to the extreme form of relation by which something is included solely through its exclusion.

The situation created in the exception has the peculiar characteristic that it cannot be defined either as a situation of fact or as a situation of right, but instead institutes a paradoxical threshold of indistinction between the two. It is not a fact, since it is only created through the suspension of the rule. But for the same reason, it is not even a juridical case in point, even if it opens the possibility of the force of law. This is the ultimate meaning of the paradox that Schmitt formulates when he writes that the sovereign decision "proves itself not to need law to create law." What is at issue in the sovereign exception is not so much the control or neutralization of an excess as the creation and definition of the very space in which the juridico-political order can have validity. In this sense, the sovereign exception is the fundamental localization (*Ortung*), which does not limit itself to distinguishing what is inside from what is outside but instead traces a threshold (the state of exception) between the two, on the basis of which outside and inside, the normal situation and chaos, enter into those complex topological relations that make the validity of the juridical order possible.

The "ordering of space" that is, according to Schmitt, constitutive of the sovereign *nomos* is therefore not only a "taking of land" (*Landesnahme*)—the determination of a juridical and a territorial ordering (of an *Ordnung* and an *Ortung*)—but above all a "taking of the outside," an exception (*Ausnahme*).

℞ Since "there is no rule that is applicable to chaos," chaos must first be included in the juridical order through the creation of a zone of indistinction between outside and inside, chaos and the normal situation— the state of exception. To refer to something, a rule must both presuppose and yet still establish a relation with what is outside relation (the nonrelational). The relation of exception thus simply expresses the originary formal structure of the juridical relation. In this sense, the sovereign decision on the exception is the originary juridico-political structure on the basis of which what is included in the juridical order and what is excluded from it acquire their meaning. In its archetypal form, the state of exception is therefore the principle of every juridical localization, since only the state of exception opens the space in which the determination of a certain juridical order and a particular territory first becomes possible. As such, the state of exception itself is thus essentially unlocalizable (even if definite spatiotemporal limits can be assigned to it from time to time). The link between localization (*Ortung*) and ordering (*Ordnung*) constitutive of the "*nomos* of the earth" (Schmitt, *Das Nomos*, p. 48) is therefore even more complex than Schmitt maintains and, at its center, contains a fundamental ambiguity, an unlocalizable zone of indistinction or exception that, in the last analysis, necessarily acts against it as a principle of its infinite dislocation. One of the theses of the present inquiry is that in our age, the state of exception comes more and more to the foreground as the fundamental political structure and ultimately begins to become the rule. When our age tried to grant the unlocalizable a permanent and visible localization, the result was the concentration camp. The camp—and not the prison—is the space that corresponds to this originary structure of the *nomos*. This is shown, among other things, by the fact that while prison law only constitutes a particular sphere of penal law and is not outside the normal order, the juridical constellation that guides the camp is (as we shall see) martial law and the state of siege. This is why it is not possible to inscribe the analysis of the camp in the trail opened by the works of Foucault, from *Madness and Civilization* to *Discipline and Punish*. As the absolute space of exception, the camp is topologically different from a simple space of confinement. And it is this space of exception, in which the link between localization and ordering is definitively broken, that has determined the crisis of the old "*nomos* of the earth."

1.3. The validity of a juridical rule does not coincide with its application to the individual case in, for example, a trial or an executive act. On the contrary, the rule must, precisely insofar as it is general, be valid independent of the individual case. Here the sphere of law shows its essential proximity to that of language. Just as in an occurrence of actual speech, a word acquires its ability to denote a segment of reality only insofar as it is also meaningful in its own not-denoting (that is, as *langue* as opposed to *parole*, as a term in its mere lexical consistency, independent of its concrete use in discourse), so the rule can refer to the individual case only because it is in force, in the sovereign exception, as pure potentiality in the suspension of every actual reference. And just as language presupposes the nonlinguistic as that with which it must maintain itself in a virtual relation (in the form of a *langue* or, more precisely, a grammatical game, that is, in the form of a discourse whose actual denotation is maintained in infinite suspension) so that it may later denote it in actual speech, so the law presupposes the nonjuridical (for example, mere violence in the form of the state of nature) as that with which it maintains itself in a potential relation in the state of exception. *The sovereign exception (as zone of indistinction between nature and right) is the presupposition of the juridical reference in the form of its suspension.* Inscribed as a presupposed exception in every rule that orders or forbids something (for example, in the rule that forbids homicide) is the pure and unsanctionable figure of the offense that, in the normal case, brings about the rule's own transgression (in the same example, the killing of a man not as natural violence but as sovereign violence in the state of exception).

א Hegel was the first to truly understand the presuppositional structure thanks to which language is at once outside and inside itself and the immediate (the nonlinguistic) reveals itself to be nothing but a presupposition of language. "Language," he wrote in the *Phenomenology of Spirit*, "is the perfect element in which interiority is as external as exteriority is internal" (see *Phänomenologie des Geistes*, pp. 527–29). We have seen that only the sovereign decision on the state of exception opens the space in which it is possible to trace borders between inside and outside and in which determinate rules can be assigned to determinate territories. In exactly the same way, only language as the pure potentiality to signify, withdrawing itself from every concrete instance of speech, divides the linguistic from the nonlinguistic and allows for the opening of areas of meaningful speech in which certain terms correspond to certain denotations. Language is the sovereign who, in a permanent state of exception, declares that there is nothing outside language and that language is always beyond itself. The particular structure of law has its foundation in this presuppositional structure of human language. It expresses the bond of inclusive exclusion to which a thing is subject because of the fact of being in language, of being named. To speak [*dire*] is, in this sense, always to "speak the law," *ius dicere*.

1.4. From this perspective, the exception is situated in a symmetrical position with respect to the example, with which it forms a system. Exception and example constitute the two modes by which a set tries to found and maintain its own coherence. But while the exception is, as we saw, an *inclusive exclusion* (which thus serves to include what is excluded), the example instead functions as an *exclusive inclusion*. Take the case of the grammatical example

(Milner, "L'exemple," p. 176): the paradox here is that a single utterance in no way distinguished from others of its kind is isolated from them precisely insofar as it belongs to them. If the syntagm "I love you" is uttered as an example of a performative speech act, then this syntagm both cannot be understood as in a normal context and yet still must be treated as a real utterance in order for it to be taken as an example. What the example shows is its belonging to a class, but for this very reason the example steps out of its class in the very moment in which it exhibits and delimits it (in the case of a linguistic syntagm, the example thus *shows* its own signifying and, in this way, suspends its own meaning). If one now asks if the rule applies to the example, the answer is not easy, since the rule applies to the example only as to a normal case and obviously not as to an example. The example is thus excluded from the normal case not because it does not belong to it but, on the contrary, because it exhibits its own belonging to it. The example is truly a *paradigm* in the etymological sense: it is what is "shown beside," and a class can contain everything except its own paradigm.

The mechanism of the exception is different. While the example is excluded from the set insofar as it belongs to it, the exception is included in the normal case precisely because it does not belong to it. And just as belonging to a class can be shown only by an example—that is, outside of the class itself—so non-belonging can be shown only at the center of the class, by an exception. In every case (as is shown by the dispute between anomalists and analogists among the ancient grammarians), exception and example are correlative concepts that are ultimately indistinguishable and that come into play every time the very sense of the belonging and commonality of individuals is to be defined. In every logical system, just as in every social system, the relation between outside and inside, strangeness and intimacy, is this complicated.

א The *exceptio* of Roman court law well shows this particular structure of the exception. The *exceptio* is an instrument of the defendant's defense that, in the case of a judgment, functions to neutralize the conclusiveness of the grounds proffered by the plaintiff and thus to render the normal application of the *ius civile* impossible. The Romans saw it as a form of exclusion directed at the application of the *ius civile* (*Digesta*, 44. 1. 2; Ulpianus, 74: *Exceptio dicta est quasi quaedam exclusio, quae opponi actioni solet ad excludendum id, quod in intentionem condemnationemve deductum est*, "It is said to be an exception because it is almost a kind of exclusion, a kind of exclusion that is usually opposed to the trial in order to exclude what was argued in the *intentio* and the *condemnatio*"). In this sense, the *exceptio* is not absolutely outside the law, but rather shows a contrast between two juridical demands, a contrast that in Roman law refers back to the opposition between *ius civile* and *ius honorarium*, that is, to the law introduced by the magistrate to temper the excessive generality of the norms of civil law.

In its technical expression in the law of the Roman court, the *exceptio* thus takes the form of a conditional negative clause inserted between the *intentio* and the *condemnatio*, by means of which the condemnation of the defendant is subordinated to the nonexistence of the fact excepted by both *intentio* and *condemnatio* (for example: *si in ea re nihil malo A. Agerii factum sit neque fiat*, "if there has not been malice"). The case of the exception is thus excluded from the application of the *ius civile* without, however, thereby calling into question the belonging of the case in point to the regulative provision. The sovereign exception represents a further dimension: it displaces a contrast between two juridical demands into a limit relation between what is inside and what is outside the law.

It may seem incongruous to define the structure of sovereign power, with its cruel factual implications, by means of two innocuous grammatical categories. Yet there is a case in which the linguistic example's decisive character and ultimate indistinguishability from the exception show an unmistakable involvement with the power of life and death. We refer to the episode in *Judges* 12: 6 in which the Galatians recognize the fleeing Ephraimites, who are trying to save themselves beyond the Jordan, by asking them to pronounce the word "Shibboleth," which the Ephraimites pronounce "Sibboleth" ("The men of Gilead said unto him, 'Art thou an Ephraimite?' If he said, 'Nay'; then they said unto him, 'Say now Shibboleth': and he said Sibboleth: for he could not frame to pronounce it right. Then they took him, and slew him at the passages of Jordan"). In the Shibboleth, example and exception become indistinguishable: "Shibboleth" is an exemplary exception or an example that functions as an exception. (In this sense, it is not surprising that there is a predilection to resort to exemplary punishment in the state of exception.)

1.5. Set theory distinguishes between membership and inclusion. A term is included when it is part of a set in the sense that all of its elements are elements of that set (one then says that b is a subset of a, and one writes it $b \subset a$). But a term may be a member of a set without being included in it (membership is, after all, the primitive notion of set theory, which one writes $b \in a$), or, conversely, a term may be included in a set without being one of its members. In a recent book, Alain Badiou has developed this distinction in order to translate it into political terms. Badiou has membership correspond to presentation, and inclusion correspond to representation (re-presentation). One then says that a term *is a member of* a situation (in political terms, these are single individuals insofar as they belong to a society). And one says that a term is *included* in a situation if it is represented in the metastructure (the State) in which the structure of the situation is counted as one term (individuals insofar as they are recodified by the State into classes, for example, or into "electorates"). Badiou defines a term as *normal* when it is both presented and represented (that is, when it both is a member and is included), as *excrescent* when it is represented but not presented (that is, when it is included in a situation without being a member of that situation), and as *singular* when it is presented but not represented (a term that is a member without being included) (*L'être*, pp. 95–115).

What becomes of the exception in this scheme? At first glance, one might think that it falls into the third case, that the exception, in other words, embodies a kind of membership without inclusion. And this is certainly Badiou's position. But what defines the character of the sovereign claim is precisely that it applies to the exception in no longer applying to it, that it includes what is outside itself. The sovereign exception is thus the figure in which singularity is represented as such, which is to say, insofar as it is unrepresentable. What cannot be included in any way is included in the form of the exception. In Badiou's scheme, the exception introduces a fourth figure, a threshold of indistinction between excrescence (representation without presentation) and singularity (presentation without representation), something like a paradoxical inclusion of membership itself. *The exception is what cannot be included in the whole of which it is a member and cannot be a member of the whole in which it is always already included.* What emerges in this limit figure is the radical crisis of every possibility of clearly distinguishing between membership and inclusion, between what is outside and what is inside, between exception and rule.

ℵ Badiou's thought is, from this perspective, a rigorous thought of the exception. His central category of the event corresponds to the structure of the exception. Badiou defines the event as an element of a situation such that its membership in the situation is undecidable from the perspective of the situation. To the State, the event thus necessarily appears as an excrescence. According to Badiou, the relation between membership and inclusion is also marked by a fundamental lack of correspondence, such that inclusion always exceeds membership (theorem of the point of excess). The exception expresses precisely this impossibility of a system's making inclusion coincide with membership, its reducing all its parts to unity.

From the point of view of language, it is possible to assimilate inclusion to sense and membership to denotation. In this way, the fact that a word always has more sense than it can actually denote corresponds to the theorem of the point of excess. Precisely this disjunction is at issue both in Claude Lévi-Strauss's theory of the constitutive excess of the signifier over the signified ("there is always a lack of equivalence between the two, which is resolvable for a divine intellect alone, and which results in the existence of a superabundance of the signifier over the signifieds on which it rests" [Introduction à Mauss, p. xlix]) and in Émile Benveniste's doctrine of the irreducible opposition between the semiotic and the semantic. The thought of our time finds itself confronted with the structure of the exception in every area. Language's sovereign claim thus consists in the attempt to make sense coincide with denotation, to stabilize a zone of indistinction between the two in which language can maintain itself in relation to its *denotata* by abandoning them and withdrawing from them into a pure *langue* (the linguistic "state of exception"). This is what deconstruction does, positing undecidables that are infinitely in excess of every possibility of signification.

1.6. This is why sovereignty presents itself in Schmitt in the form of a decision on the exception. Here the decision is not the expression of the will of a subject hierarchically superior to all others, but rather represents the inscription within the body of the *nomos* of the exteriority that animates it and gives it meaning. The sovereign decides not the licit and illicit but the originary inclusion of the living in the sphere of law or, in the words of Schmitt, "the normal structuring of life relations," which the law needs. The decision concerns neither a *quaestio iuris* nor a *quaestio facti,* but rather the very relation between law and fact. Here it is a question not only, as Schmitt seems to suggest, of the irruption of the "effective life" that, in the exception, "breaks the crust of a mechanism grown rigid through repetition" but of something that concerns the most inner nature of the law. The law has a regulative character and is a "rule" not because it commands and proscribes, but because it must first of all create the sphere of its own reference in real life and *make that reference regular.* Since the rule both stabilizes and pre-supposes the conditions of this reference, the originary structure of the rule is always of this kind: "If (a real case in point, e.g.: *si membrum rupsit*), then (juridical consequence, e.g.: *talio esto*)," in which a fact is included in the juridical order through its exclusion, and transgression seems to precede and determine the lawful case. That the law initially has the form of a *lex talionis* (*talio,* perhaps from *talis,* amounts to "the thing itself") means that the juridical order does not originally present itself simply as sanctioning a transgressive fact but instead constitutes itself through the repetition of the same act without any sanction, that is, as an exceptional case. This is not a punishment of this first act, but rather represents its inclusion in the juridical order, violence as a primordial juridical fact (*permittit enim lex parem vindictam,* "for the law allows equitable vengeance" [Pompeius Festus, *De verborum significatione,* 496. 15]). In this sense, the exception is the originary form of law.

The cipher of this capture of life in law is not sanction (which is not at all an exclusive characteristic of the juridical rule) but guilt (not in the technical sense that this concept has in penal law but in the originary sense that indicates a being-in-debt: *in culpa esse*), which is to say, precisely the condition of being included through an exclusion, of being in relation to something from which one is excluded or which one cannot fully assume. *Guilt refers not to transgression, that is, to the determination of the licit and the illicit, but to the pure force of the law, to the law's simple reference to something.* This is the ultimate ground of the juridical maxim, which is foreign to all morality, according to which ignorance of the rule does not eliminate guilt. In this impossibility of deciding if it is guilt that grounds the rule or the rule that posits guilt, what comes clearly to light is the indistinction between outside and inside and between life and law that characterizes the sovereign decision on the exception. The "sovereign" structure of the law, its peculiar and original "force," has the form of a state of exception in which fact and law are indistinguishable (yet must, nevertheless, be decided on). Life, which is thus obliged, can in the last instance be implicated in the sphere of law only through the presupposition of its inclusive exclusion, only in an *exceptio.* There is a limit-figure of life, a threshold in which life is both inside and outside the juridical order, and this threshold is the place of sovereignty.

The statement "The rule lives off the exception alone" must therefore be taken to the letter. Law is made of nothing but what it manages to capture inside itself through the inclusive exclusion of the *exceptio*: it nourishes itself on this exception and is a dead letter without it. In this sense, the law truly "has no existence in itself, but rather has its being in the very life of men." The sovereign decision traces and from time to time renews this threshold of indistinction between outside and inside, exclusion and inclusion, *nomos* and *physis*, in which life is originarily excepted in law. Its decision is the position of an undecidable.

ℵ Not by chance is Schmitt's first work wholly devoted to the definition of the juridical concept of guilt. What is immediately striking in this study is the decision with which the author refutes every technico-formal definition of the concept of guilt in favor of terms that, at first glance, seem more moral than juridical. Here, in fact, guilt is (against the ancient juridical proverb "There is no guilt without rule") first of all a "process of inner life," which is to say, something essentially "intrasubjective," which can be qualified as a real "ill will" that consists in "knowingly positing ends contrary to those of the juridical order" (*Über Schuld*, pp. 18–24, 92).

It is not possible to say whether Benjamin was familiar with this text while he was writing "Fate and Character" and "Critique of Violence." But it remains the case that his definition of guilt as an originary juridical concept unduly transferred to the ethico-religious sphere is in perfect agreement with Schmitt's thesis—even if Benjamin's definition goes in a decisively opposed direction. For Benjamin, the state of demonic existence of which law is a residue is to be overcome and man is to be liberated from guilt (which is nothing other than the inscription of natural life in the order of law and destiny). At the heart of the Schmittian assertion of the juridical character and centrality of the notion of guilt is, however, not the freedom of the ethical man but only the controlling force of a sovereign power (*katechon*), which can, in the best of cases, merely slow the dominion of the Antichrist.

There is an analogous convergence with respect to the concept of character. Like Benjamin, Schmitt clearly distinguishes between character and guilt ("the concept of guilt," he writes, "has to do with an *operari*, and not with an *esse*" [*Über Schuld*, p. 46]). Yet in Benjamin, it is precisely this element (character insofar as it escapes all conscious willing) that presents itself as the principle capable of releasing man from guilt and of affirming natural innocence.

1.7. If the exception is the structure of sovereignty, then sovereignty is not an exclusively political concept, an exclusively juridical category, a power external to law (Schmitt), or the supreme rule of the juridical order (Hans Kelsen): it is the originary structure in which law refers to life and includes it in itself by suspending it. Taking up Jean-Luc Nancy's suggestion, we shall give the name *ban* (from the old Germanic term that designates both exclusion from the community and the command and insignia of the sovereign) to this potentiality (in the proper sense of the Aristotelian *dynamis*, which is always also *dynamis mē energein*, the potentiality not to pass into actuality) of the law to maintain itself in its own privation, to apply in no longer applying. The relation of exception is a relation of ban. He who has been banned is not, in fact, simply set outside the law and made indifferent to it but rather *abandoned* by it, that is, exposed and threatened on the threshold in which life and law, outside and inside, become indistinguishable. It is literally not possible to say whether the one who has been banned is outside or inside the juridical order. (This is why in Romance languages, to be "banned" originally means both to be "at the mercy of" and "at one's own will, freely," to be "excluded" and also "open to all, free.") It is in this sense that the paradox of sovereignty can take the form "There is nothing outside the law." *The originary relation of law to life is not application but Abandonment.* The matchless potentiality of the *nomos, its originary "force of law,"* is that it holds life in its ban by abandoning it. This is the structure of the ban that we shall try to understand here, so that we can eventually call it into question.

א The ban is a form of relation. But precisely what kind of relation is at issue here, when the ban has no positive content and the terms of the relation seem to exclude (and, at the same time, to include) each other? What is the form of law that expresses itself in the ban? The ban is the pure form of reference to something in general, which is to say, the simple positing of relation with the nonrelational. In this sense, the ban is identical with the limit form of relation. A critique of the ban will therefore necessarily have to put the very form of relation into question, and to ask if the political fact is not perhaps thinkable beyond relation and, thus, no longer in the form of a connection.

§ 2 'Nomos Basileus'

2.1. The principle according to which sovereignty belongs to law, which today seems inseparable from our conception of democracy and the legal State, does not at all eliminate the paradox of sovereignty; indeed it even brings it to the most extreme point of its development. Since the most ancient recorded formulation of this principle, Pindar's fragment 169, the sovereignty of law has been situated in a dimension so dark and ambiguous that it has prompted scholars to speak quite rightly of an "enigma" (Ehrenberg, *Rechtsidee*, p. 119). Here is the text of the fragment reconstructed by Boeck:

> Nomos ho pantōn basileus
> thnatōn te kai athanatōn
> agei dikaiōn to Biaiotaton
> hypertatai cheiri: tekmairomai
> ergoisin Herakleos.

> The *nomos*, sovereign of all,
> Of mortals and immortals,
> Leads with the strongest hand,
> Justifying the most violent.
> I judge this from the works of Hercules.

The enigma consists in more than the fact that there are many possible interpretations of the fragment. What is decisive is that the poet—as the reference to Hercules' theft clarifies beyond the shadow of a doubt—defines the sovereignty of the *nomos* by means of a justification of violence. The fragment's meaning becomes clear only when one understands that at its center lies a scandalous unification of the two essentially antithetical principles that the Greeks called *Bia* and *Dikē*, violence and justice. *Nomos* is the power that, "with the strongest hand," achieves the paradoxical union of these opposites (in this sense, if one understands an enigma in the Aristotelian sense, as a "conjunction of opposites," the fragment truly does contain an enigma).

If in Solon's fragment 24 one should read (as most scholars maintain) *kratei nomou*, then already in the sixth century the specific "force" of law was identified precisely in a "connection" of violence and justice (*kratei/nomou bian te kai dikēn synarmosas*, "with the force of the *nomos* I have connected violence and justice"; but even if one reads *homou* instead of *nomou*, the central idea remains the same once Solon speaks of his activity as legislator [see De Romilly, *La loi*, p. 15]). A passage from Hesiod's *Works and Days*, which Pindar may have had in mind, also assigns a decisive position to the relation between violence and law:

> O Perseus, keep these things in mind and
> forget violence [*Biaia*] when you attend to justice [*Dikē*].
> To men, Zeus gave this *nomos*:
> what is proper to the fish, the wild beasts, and the winged birds
> is to devour each other, since there is no *Dikē* between them.
> But to men Zeus gave *Dikē*, which is much better.

While in Hesiod the *nomos* is still the power that divides violence from law and, with it, the world of beasts from the world of men, and while in Solon the "connection" of *Bia* and *Dikē* contains neither ambiguity nor irony, in Pindar—and this is the knot that he bequeaths to Western political thought and that makes him, in a certain sense, the first great thinker of sovereignty—*the sovereign nomos is the principle that, joining law and violence, threatens them with indistinction.* In this sense, Pindar's fragment on the *nomos basileus* contains the hidden paradigm guiding every successive definition of sovereignty: the sovereign is the point of indistinction between violence and law, the threshold on which violence passes over into law and law passes over into violence.

א This is how Friedrich Hölderlin (who most likely had before him a text that had been emended in accordance with the Platonic citation in the *Gorgias*: *Biaiōn ton dikaiotaton*, "Doing violence to the most just" [484b, 1–10]) translates the fragment in his annotated version of Pindar's fragments (which Friedrich Beißner dates at 1803):

Das Höchste

Das Gesetz,
Von allen der König, Sterblichen und
Unsterblichen; das führt eben
Darum gewaltig
Das gerechteste Recht mit allerhöchster Hand.

The Highest

The law,
Sovereign of all, mortals and
Immortals; this is why
It leads, violently,
The most just justice with the supreme hand.

In the name of his theory of the constitutive superiority of the *nomos* over law (*Gesetz*, in the sense of conventional positing), Schmitt criticizes the Hölderlinian interpretation of the fragment. "Even Hölderlin," Schmitt writes, "is mistaken in his translation of the fragment . . . , since he renders the term *nomos* with *Gesetz* and lets himself be misled by this unfortunate word even though he knows that law is rigorous mediacy. The *nomos* in the originary sense is, rather, the pure immediacy of a juridical power [*Rechtskraft*] not mediated by law. It is a constitutive historical event, an act of legitimacy that alone renders the legality of the new law meaningful in general" (*Das Nomos*, p. 42).

Here Schmitt completely misinterprets the intention of the poet, which is directed precisely against every immediate principle. In his commentary, Hölderlin defines the *nomos* (which he distinguishes from law) as rigorous mediation (*strenge Mittelbarkeit*): "The immediate," he writes, "is, taken in the rigorous sense, impossible for mortals as for immortals; the god must distinguish different worlds, according to his nature, since the heavenly goods must be holy for themselves, unmixed. Insofar as he knows, man too must distinguish different worlds, since knowledge is only possible through opposition" (*Sämtliche Werke*, p. 309). If Hölderlin (like Schmitt) sees a principle higher than simple law in the *nomos basileus*, nonetheless he is careful to specify that the term "sovereign" refers here not to a "supreme power" (*höchste Macht*) but to the "highest ground of knowledge" (ibid.). With one of those corrections so characteristic of his last translations, Hölderlin thus displaces a juridico-political problem (the sovereignty of law as the indistinction of law and violence) into the sphere of the theory of knowledge (mediation as the power of distinguishing). What is more original and stronger than law is not (as in Schmitt) the *nomos* as sovereign principle but rather the mediation that grounds knowledge.

2.2. It is in this light that we must read the Platonic citation in the *Gorgias* (484b, 1–10), which, while appearing as simple forgetfulness, consciously alters the Pindaric text:

Even Pindar, it seems to me, has held what I think in the verses in which he says:

the *nomos*, sovereign of all
mortals and immortals

And this is how Plato's text then continues:

Leads with the strongest hand
Doing violence to the most just.

Only an acute *coniunctivitis professoria* was able to induce philologists (in particular, the editor of the now aged Oxonian critical edition of Plato) to correct the more authoritative manuscripts' phrase, *biaiōn to dikaiotaton*, in accordance with the letter of Pindar's text (*dikaiōn to biaiotaton*). As Ulrich von Wilamowitz-Möllendorf has justly observed (*Platon*, pp. 95–97), *biaiōn* is too rare in Greek to be explained by a lapse of memory (let alone a *lapsus calami*), and the meaning of the Platonic wordplay is perfectly clear: here the "justification of violence" is at the same time a "doing violence to the most just," and the "sovereignty" of the *nomos* of which Pindar speaks consists in this and nothing else.

An analogous intention guides the implicit citation that Plato, in the *Protagoras*, puts in the mouth of Hippias: "You people who are present, I maintain that you are all relatives, neighbors, and citizens by nature and not by law. The similar is related to the similar by nature, but the *nomos*, the tyrant [*tyrannos*, not *basileus*] of men, commits many acts of violence against nature" (337c). This intention also guides the explicit citation in *The Laws*:

> [The axiom according to which it is the strongest who rules] is, as the Theban Pindar said, by nature extremely common among all living beings. But the axiom that seems to be more important is the sixth one, which is to say, the one that orders that he who knows and is intelligent should govern, and that the ignorant should therefore follow him. And you will not be able to say that this, wise Pindar, happens against nature, for it happens not by means of violence but in accordance with nature, that is, in accordance with the power of law over those who accept it. (690b–c)

In both cases, what interests Plato is not so much the opposition between *physis* and *nomos*, which had been at the center of the Sophists' debate (Stier, "Nomos basileus," pp. 245–46), as the coincidence of violence and law constitutive of sovereignty. In the passage from *The Laws* cited above, the power of law is defined as being in accordance with nature (*kata physin*) and essentially nonviolent because Plato is most of all concerned to neutralize the opposition that, for both the Sophists and Pindar (in a different way), justified the "sovereign" confusion of *Bia* and *Dikē*.

The entire treatment of the problem of the relation between *physis* and *nomos* in the tenth book of *The Laws* is undertaken to dismantle the Sophistic construction of this opposition as well as the thesis of the anteriority of nature with respect to law. Plato neutralizes both by affirming the originarity of the soul and of "all that belongs to what is a soul" (intellect, *technē*, and *nomos*) with respect to bodies and the elements "that we erroneously say are in accordance with nature" (892b). When Plato (and with him, all the representatives of what Leo Strauss calls "classical natural right") says that "law must rule over men, and not men over law," he therefore means to affirm not law's sovereignty over nature but, on the contrary, its "natural," which is to say nonviolent, character. While in Plato the "law of nature" is thus born to undermine the Sophistic opposition of *physis* and *nomos* and to exclude the sovereign confusion of violence and law, in the Sophists the opposition serves precisely to found the principle of sovereignty, the union of *Bia* and *Dikē*.

2.3. The very sense of this opposition, which has had such a tenacious lineage in the political culture of the West, will be considered here in a new way. The Sophistic polemic against *nomos* in favor of nature (which developed with ever-increasing urgency during the course of the fourth century) can be considered the necessary premise of the opposition between the state of nature and the "commonwealth,"[1] which Hobbes posits as the ground of his conception of sovereignty. If for the Sophists the anteriority of *physis* ultimately justifies the violence of the strongest, for Hobbes it is this very identity of the state of nature and violence (*homo hominis lupus*) that justifies the absolute power of the sovereign. In both cases, even if in an apparently opposed fashion, the *physis/ nomos* antinomy constitutes the presupposition that legitimates the principle of sovereignty, the indistinction of law and violence (in the Sophists' strong man or Hobbes's sovereign). It is important to note that in Hobbes the state of nature survives in the person of the sovereign, who is the only one to preserve its natural *ius contra omnes*. Sovereignty thus presents itself as an incorporation of the state of nature in society, or, if one prefers, as a state of indistinction between nature and culture, between violence and law, and this very indistinction constitutes specifically sovereign violence. The state of nature is therefore not truly external to *nomos* but rather contains its virtuality. The state of nature (certainly in the modern era, but probably also in that of the Sophists) is the being-in-potentiality [*l'essere-in-potenza*] of the law, the law's self-

1. In English in the original.—Trans.

presupposition as "natural law." Hobbes, after all, was perfectly aware, as Strauss has underscored, that the state of nature did not necessarily have to be conceived as a real epoch, but rather could be understood as a principle internal to the State revealed in the moment in which the State is considered "as if it were dissolved" (*ut tanquam dissoluta consideretur* [Hobbes, *De cive*, pp. 79–80]). Exteriority—the law of nature and the principle of the preservation of one's own life—is truly the innermost center of the political system, and the political system lives off it in the same way that the rule, according to Schmitt, lives off the exception.

2.4. From this perspective, it will not seem surprising that Schmitt grounds his theory of the originary character of the "*nomos* of the earth*" precisely on Pindar's fragment and, nevertheless, makes no allusion to his own definition of sovereignty as the decision on the state of exception. What Schmitt wishes to establish above all is the superiority of the sovereign *nomos* as the constitutive event of law with respect to every positivistic conception of law as simple position and convention (*Gesetz*). This is why Schmitt must leave the essential proximity between *nomos* and the state of exception in obscurity, even though he speaks of "sovereign *nomos.*" And yet a more attentive reading reveals that this proximity is clearly present. A little later, in the chapter "First Global Lines," Schmitt shows how the link between localization and ordering constitutive of the *nomos* of the earth always implies a zone that is excluded from law and that takes the shape of a "free and juridically empty space" in which the sovereign power no longer knows the limits fixed by the *nomos* as the territorial order. In the classical epoch of the *ius publicum Europaeum*, this zone corresponded to the New World, which was identified with the state of nature in which everything is possible (Locke: "In the beginning, all the world was America"). Schmitt himself assimilates this zone "beyond the line"[2] to the state of exception, which "bases itself in an obviously analogous fashion on the idea of delimited,

2. In English in the original.—Trans.

free and empty space" understood as a "temporary and spatial sphere in which every law is suspended":

It was, however, delimited with respect to the normal legal system: in time, at first through the declaration of the state of war and, in the end, through an act of indemnity; in space, by a precise indication of its sphere of validity. Inside this spatial and temporal sphere, anything could happen as long as it was held to be de facto necessary according to circumstances. There is an ancient and obvious symbol of this situation, to which Montesquieu also makes reference: the statue of freedom or of justice was veiled for a determinate period of time. (Schmitt, *Das Nomos*, p. 67)

Insofar as it is sovereign, the *nomos* is necessarily connected with both the state of nature and the state of exception. The state of exception (with its necessary indistinction of *Bia* and *Dikē*) is not external to the *nomos* but rather, even in its clear delimitation, included in the *nomos* as a moment that is in every sense funda-mental. At its very center, the localization-ordering link thus al-ways already contains its own virtual rupture in the form of a "suspension of every law." But what then appears (at the point in which society is considered as *tanquam dissoluta*) is in fact not the state of nature (as an earlier stage into which men would fall back) but the state of exception. The state of nature and the state of exception are nothing but two sides of a single topological process in which what was presupposed as external (the state of nature) now reappears, as in a Möbius strip or a Leyden jar, in the inside (as state of exception), and the sovereign power is this very impos-sibility of distinguishing between outside and inside, nature and exception, *physis* and *nomos*. The state of exception is thus not so much a spatiotemporal suspension as a complex topological figure in which not only the exception and the rule but also the state of nature and law, outside and inside, pass through one another. It is precisely this topological zone of indistinction, which had to re-main hidden from the eyes of justice, that we must try to fix under our gaze. The process (which Schmitt carefully described and which we are still living) that began to become apparent in the First

World War, through which the constitutive link between the localization and ordering of the old *nomos* was broken and the entire
system of the reciprocal limitations and rules of the *ius publicum
Europaeum* brought to ruin, has its hidden ground in the sovereign
exception. What happened and is still happening before our eyes is
that the "juridically empty" space of the state of exception (in
which law is in force in the figure—that is, etymologically, in the
fiction—of its own dissolution, and in which everything that the
sovereign deemed de facto necessary could happen) has trans-
gressed its spatiotemporal boundaries and now, overflowing outside them, is starting to coincide with the normal order, in which
everything again becomes possible.

ℵ If one wanted to represent schematically the relation between the
state of nature and the state of law that takes shape in the state of
exception, one could have recourse to two circles that at first appear to be
distinct (Fig. 1) but later, in the state of exception, show themselves to be
in fact inside each other (Fig. 2). When the exception starts to become
the rule, the two circles coincide in absolute indistinction (Fig. 3).

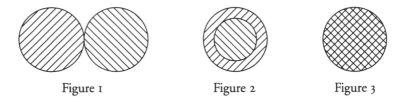

Figure 1   Figure 2   Figure 3

From this perspective, what is happening in ex-Yugoslavia and, more
generally, what is happening in the processes of dissolution of traditional
State organisms in Eastern Europe should be viewed not as a reemergence
of the natural state of struggle of all against all—which functions as a pre-
lude to new social contracts and new national and State localizations—
but rather as the coming to light of the state of exception as the permanent structure of juridico-political de-localization and dis-location.
Political organization is not regressing toward outdated forms; rather,
premonitory events are, like bloody masses, announcing the new *nomos*
of the earth, which (if its grounding principle is not called into question)
will soon extend itself over the entire planet.

§ 3 Potentiality and Law

3.1. Perhaps nowhere else does the paradox of sovereignty show itself so fully as in the problem of constituting power and its relation to constituted power. Both theory and positive legislation have always encountered difficulties in formulating and maintaining this distinction in all its weight. "The reason for this," a recent treatise of political science reads,

> is that if one really means to give the distinction between constituting power and constituted power its true meaning, it is necessary to place constituting and constituted power on two different levels. Constituted powers exist only *in* the State: inseparable from a preestablished constitutional order, they need the State frame, whose reality they manifest. Constituting power, on the other hand, is situated *outside* the State; it owes nothing to the State, it exists without it, it is the spring whose current no use can ever exhaust. (Burdeau, *Traité*, p. 173)

Hence the impossibility of harmoniously constructing the relation between the two powers—an impossibility that emerges in particular not only when one attempts to understand the juridical nature of dictatorship and of the state of exception, but also when the text of constitutions themselves foresees, as it often does, the power of revision. Today, in the context of the general tendency to regulate everything by means of rules, fewer and fewer are willing to claim that constituting power is originary and irreducible, that it cannot be conditioned and constrained in any way by a determinate legal system and that it necessarily maintains itself outside every constituted power. The power from which the constitution is born is increasingly dismissed as a prejudice or a merely factual matter, and constituting power is more and more frequently reduced to the power of revision foreseen in the constitution.

As early as the end of the First World War, Benjamin criticized this tendency with words that have lost none of their currency. He presented the relation between constituting power and constituted power as the relation between the violence that posits law and the violence that preserves it:

> If the awareness of the latent presence of violence in a legal institution disappears, the juridical institution decays. An example of this is provided today by the parliaments. They present such a well-known, sad spectacle because they have not remained aware of the revolutionary forces to which they owe their existence. . . . They lack a sense of the creative violence of law that is represented in them. One need not then be surprised that they do not arrive at decisions worthy of this violence, but instead oversee a course of political affairs that avoids violence through compromise. (Benjamin, "Zur Kritik der Gewalt," p. 144)

But the other position (that of the democratico-revolutionary tradition), which wants to maintain constituting power in its sovereign transcendence with respect to every constituted order, threatens to remain just as imprisoned within the paradox that we have tried to describe until now. For if constituting power is, as the violence that posits law, certainly more noble than the violence that preserves it, constituting power still possesses no title that might legitimate something other than law-preserving violence and even maintains an ambiguous and ineradicable relation with constituted power.

From this perspective, Emmanuel-Joseph Sieyès's famous statement, "The constitution first of all presupposes a constituting power," is not, as has been claimed, a simple truism: it must rather be understood in the sense that *the constitution presupposes itself as constituting power* and, in this form, expresses the paradox of sovereignty in the most telling way. Just as sovereign power presupposes itself as the state of nature, which is thus maintained in a relation of ban with the state of law, so the sovereign power divides itself into constituting power and constituted power and maintains itself in relation to both, positioning itself at their point of indistinction. Sieyès himself was so conscious of this implication as to place constituting power (identified in the "nation") in a state of nature outside the social tie: "One must think of the nations of the earth," he writes, "as individuals, outside the social tie . . . in the state of nature" (Sieyès, *Qu'est ce que le Tiers État?*, p. 83).

3.2. Hannah Arendt, who cites this line in *On Revolution*, describes how sovereignty was demanded in the course of the French Revolution in the form of an absolute principle capable of founding the legislative act of constituting power. And she shows well how this demand (which is also present in Robespierre's idea of a Supreme Being) ultimately winds up in a vicious circle:

> What he [Robespierre] needed was by no means just a "Supreme Being"—a term which was not his—he needed rather what he himself called an "Immortal Legislator" and what, in a different context, he also named a "continuous appeal to Justice." In terms of the French Revolution, he needed an ever-present transcendent source of authority that could not be identified with the general will of either the nation or the Revolution itself, so that an absolute Sovereignty—Blackstone's "despotic power"—might bestow sovereignty upon the nation, that an absolute Immortality might guarantee, if not immortality, then at least some permanence and stability to the republic. (Arendt, *On Revolution*, p. 185)

Here the basic problem is not so much how to conceive a constituting power that does not exhaust itself in a constituted power (which is not easy, but still theoretically resolvable), as how clearly to differentiate constituting from constituted power, which is surely a more difficult problem. Attempts to think the preservation of constituting power are certainly not lacking in our age, and they have become familiar to us through the Trotskyite notion of a "permanent revolution" and the Maoist concept of "uninterrupted revolution." Even the power of councils (which there is no reason not to think of as stable, even if de facto constituted revolutionary powers have done everything in their power to eliminate them) can, from this perspective, be considered as a survival of constituting power within constituted power. But the two great destroyers of spontaneous councils in our time—the Leninist party and the Nazi party—also present themselves, in a certain sense, as the preservers of a constituting moment [*istanza*] alongside constituted power. It is in this light that we ought to consider the characteristic "dual" structure of the great totalitarian states of our century (the Soviet Union and Nazi Germany), which has made things so difficult for historians of public law. The structure by which the State party tends to appear as a duplicate of the State structure can then be considered as a paradoxical and interesting technico-juridical solution to the problem of how to maintain constituting power. Yet it is just as certain that in both of these cases, constituting power either appears as the expression of a sovereign power or does not let itself easily be separated from sovereign power. The analogy between the Soviet Union and the Nazi Reich is even more compelling insofar as in both cases, the question "Where?" is the essential one once neither the constituting power nor the sovereign can be situated wholly inside or altogether outside the constituted order.

ℵ Schmitt considers constituting power as a "political will" capable of "making the concrete, fundamental decision on the nature and form of one's own political existence." As such, constituting power stands "before and above every constitutional legislative procedure" and is irreducible to the level of juridical rules as well as theoretically distinct from sovereign power (*Verfassungslehre*, pp. 75–76). But if constituting power is identified with the constituting will of the people or the nation, as already happens (according to Schmitt) with Sieyès, then the criterion that makes it possible to distinguish constituting power from popular or national sovereignty becomes unclear, and the constituting subject and the sovereign subject begin to become indistinguishable. Schmitt criticizes the liberal attempt to "contain and delimit the use of state power by means of written laws," and he affirms the sovereignty of the constitution or the fundamental *charte*: the instances competent for the revision of the constitution "do not, following this competence, become either sovereign or titular of a constituting power" (ibid., pp. 107–8). From this perspective, both constituting power and sovereign power exceed the level of the juridical rule (even of the fundamental juridical rule), but the symmetry of this excess attests to a proximity that fades away into indistinction.

In a recent book, Antonio Negri has undertaken to show the irreducibility of constituting power (defined as "the praxis of a constituting act, renewed in freedom, organized in the continuity of a free praxis") to every form of constituted order, and, at the same time, to deny that constituting power is reducible to the principle of sovereignty. "The truth of constituting power," he writes,

> is not the one that can (in any way whatsoever) be attributed to the concept of sovereignty. This is not the truth of constituting power not only because constituting power is not (as is obvious) an emanation of constituted power, but also because constituting power is not the institution of constituted power: it is the act of choice, the punctual determination that opens a horizon, the radical enacting of something that did not exist before and whose conditions of existence stipulate that the creative act cannot lose its characteristics in creating. When constituting power sets the constituting process in motion, every determination is free and remains free. Sovereignty, on the other hand, arises as the establishment—and therefore as the end—of constituting power, as the consumption of the freedom brought by constituting power. (Negri, *Il potere costituente*, p. 31)

The problem of the difference between constituting power and sovereign power is, certainly, essential. Yet the fact that constituting power neither derives from the constituted order nor limits itself to instituting it—being, rather, free praxis—still says nothing as to constituting power's alterity with respect to sovereign power. If our analysis of the original ban-structure of sovereignty is exact, these attributes do indeed belong to sovereign power, and Negri cannot find any criterion, in his wide analysis of the historical phenomenology of constituting power, by which to isolate constituting power from sovereign power.

The strength of Negri's book lies instead in the final perspective

it opens insofar as it shows how constituting power, when conceived in all its radicality, ceases to be a strictly political concept
and necessarily presents itself as a category of ontology. The problem of constituting power then becomes the problem of the "constitution of potentiality" (*Il potere costituente*, p.

383), and the
unresolved dialectic between constituting power and constituted
power opens the way for a new articulation of the relation between
potentiality and actuality, which requires nothing less than a re-
thinking of the ontological categories of modality in their totality.
The problem is therefore moved from political philosophy to first
philosophy (or, if one likes, politics is returned to its ontological
position). Only an entirely new conjunction of possibility and
reality, contingency and necessity, and the other *pathē tou ontos*,
will make it possible to cut the knot that binds sovereignty to
constituting power. And only if it is possible to think the relation
between potentiality and actuality differently—and even to think
beyond this relation—will it be possible to think a constituting
power wholly released from the sovereign ban. Until a new and
coherent ontology of potentiality (beyond the steps that have been
made in this direction by Spinoza, Schelling, Nietzsche, and Heidegger) has replaced the ontology founded on the primacy of
actuality and its relation to potentiality, a political theory freed
from the aporias of sovereignty remains unthinkable.

3.3. The relation between constituting power and constituted
power is just as complicated as the relation Aristotle establishes
between potentiality and act, *dynamis* and *energeia;* and, in the last
analysis, the relation between constituting and constituted power
(perhaps like every authentic understanding of the problem of
sovereignty) depends on how one thinks the existence and auton-
omy of potentiality. According to Aristotle's thought, potentiality
precedes actuality and conditions it, but also seems to remain
essentially subordinate to it. Against the Megarians, who (like those
politicians today who want to reduce all constituting power to
constituted power) affirm that potentiality exists only in act (*energē
monon dynasthai*), Aristotle always takes great care to affirm the

autonomous existence of potentiality—the fact that the kithara player keeps his ability [*potenza*] to play even when he does not play, and that the architect keeps his ability [*potenza*] to build even when he does not build. What Aristotle undertakes to consider in Book Theta of the *Metaphysics* is, in other words, not potentiality as a merely logical possibility but rather the effective modes of potentiality's existence. This is why, if potentiality is to have its own consistency and not always disappear immediately into actuality, it is necessary that potentiality be able *not* to pass over into actuality, that potentiality constitutively be the *potentiality not to* (do or be), or, as Aristotle says, that potentiality be also im-potentiality (*adynamia*). Aristotle decisively states this principle—which, in a certain sense, is the cardinal point on which his entire theory of *dynamis* turns—in a lapidary formula: "Every potentiality is impotentiality of the same and with respect to the same" (*tou autou kai kata to auto pasa dynamis adynamiai*) (*Metaphysics*, 1046a, 32). Or, even more explicitly: "What is potential can both be and not be. For the same is potential as much with respect to being as to not being" (*to dynaton endekhetai kai einai kai mē einai*) (1050b, 10).

The potentiality that exists is precisely the potentiality that can not pass over into actuality (this is why Avicenna, faithful to the Aristotelian intention, calls it "the perfect potentiality" and chooses as its example the figure of the scribe in the moment in which he does not write). This potentiality maintains itself in relation to actuality in the form of its suspension; it *is capable* of the act in not realizing it, it is sovereignly capable of its own im-potentiality [*impotenza*]. But how, from this perspective, to think the passage into actuality? If every potentiality (to be or do) is also originarily the potentiality not to (be or do), how will it be possible for an act to be realized?

Aristotle's answer is contained in a definition that constitutes one of the most acute testimonies to his genius and that has for this very reason often been misunderstood: "A thing is said to be potential if, when the act of which it is said to be potential is realized, there will be nothing im-potential (that is, there will be nothing able not to be)" (*Metaphysics*, 1047a, 24–26). The last three words of the definition (*ouden estai adynaton*) do not mean, as the usual and completely trivializing reading maintains, "there will be nothing impossible" (that is, what is not impossible is possible). They specify, rather, the condition into which potentiality—which can both be and not be—can realize itself. What is potential can pass over into actuality only at the point at which it sets aside its own potential not to be (its *adynamia*). To set im-potentiality aside is not to destroy it but, on the contrary, to fulfill it, to turn potentiality back upon itself in order to give itself to itself. In a passage of *De anima*, Aristotle expresses the nature of perfect potentiality perhaps most fully, and he describes the passage to actuality (in the case of the *technai* and human skills, which also stands at the center of Book Theta of the *Metaphysics*) not as an alteration or destruction of potentiality in actuality but as a preservation and "giving of the self to itself" of potentiality:

> To suffer is not a simple term, but is in one sense a certain destruction through the opposite principle and, in another sense, the preservation [*sōtēria*, salvation] of what is in potentiality by what is in actuality and what is similar to it. . . . For he who possesses science [in potentiality] becomes someone who contemplates in actuality, and either this is not an alteration—since here there is the gift of the self to itself and to actuality [*epidosis eis eauto*]—or this is an alteration of a different kind. (*De anima*, 417b, 2–16)

In thus describing the most authentic nature of potentiality, Aristotle actually bequeathed the paradigm of sovereignty to Western philosophy. For the sovereign ban, which applies to the exception in no longer applying, corresponds to the structure of potentiality, which maintains itself in relation to actuality precisely through its ability not to be. Potentiality (in its double appearance as potentiality to and as potentiality not to) is that through which Being founds itself *sovereignly*, which is to say, without anything preceding or determining it (*superiorem non recognoscens*) other than its own ability not to be. And an act is sovereign when it realizes itself by simply taking away its own potentiality not to be, letting itself be, giving itself to itself.

Hence the constitutive ambiguity of the Aristotelian theory of *dynamis/energeia*: if it is never clear, to a reader freed from the prejudices of tradition, whether Book Theta of the *Metaphysics* in fact gives primacy to actuality or to potentiality, this is not because of a certain indecisiveness or, worse, contradiction in the philoso- pher's thought but because potentiality and actuality are simply the two faces of the sovereign self-grounding of Being. Sovereignty is always double because Being, as potentiality, suspends itself, main- taining itself in a relation of ban (or abandonment) with itself in order to realize itself as absolute actuality (which thus presupposes nothing other than its own potentiality). At the limit, pure poten- tiality and pure actuality are indistinguishable, and the sovereign is precisely this zone of indistinction. (In Aristotle's *Metaphysics*, this corresponds to the figure of the "thinking of thinking," that is, to a thinking that in actuality thinks its own potentiality to think.)

This is why it is so hard to think both a "constitution of potentiality" entirely freed from the principle of sovereignty and a constituting power that has definitively broken the ban binding it to constituted power. That constituting power never exhausts itself in constituted power is not enough: sovereign power can also, as such, maintain itself indefinitely, without ever passing over into actuality. (The troublemaker is precisely the one who tries to force sovereign power to translate itself into actuality.) Instead one must think the existence of potentiality without any relation to Being in the form of actuality—not even in the extreme form of the ban and the potentiality not to be, and of actuality as the fulfillment and manifestation of potentiality—and think the existence of poten- tiality even without any relation to being in the form of the gift of the self and of letting be. This, however, implies nothing less than thinking ontology and politics beyond every figure of relation, beyond even the limit relation that is the sovereign ban. Yet it is this very task that many, today, refuse to assume at any cost.

ℵ It has already been noted that a principle of potentiality is inherent in every definition of sovereignty. In this sense, Gérard Mairet observed that the sovereign state is founded on an "ideology of potentiality" that consists in "leading the two elements of every power back to a unity . . . the principle of potentiality and the form of its exercise" (*Histoire*, p. 289). The central idea here is that "potentiality already exists before it is exercised, and that obedience precedes the institutions that make it possible" (ibid., p. 311). That this ideology truly has a mythological character is suggested by the same author: "It is a question of a real myth whose secrets we still do not know, but which constitutes, perhaps, the secret of every power." It is the structure of this mystery [*arcano*] that we have undertaken to bring to light in the figure of abandonment and the "potentiality not to." But here we run up against not a mythologeme in the strict sense but, rather, the ontological root of every political power. (Potentiality and actuality are, for Aristotle, first of all categories of being, two ways "in which Being is said.")

In modern thought, there are rare but significant attempts to conceive of being beyond the principle of sovereignty. In the *Philosophy of Revelation*, Schelling thus thinks an absolute entity that presupposes no potentiality and never exists *per transitum de potentia ad actum*. In the late Nietzsche, the eternal return of the same gives form to the impossibility of distinguishing between potentiality and actuality, even as the *Amor fati* gives shape to the impossibility of distinguishing between contingency and necessity. In the Heideggerian idea of abandonment and the *Ereignis*, it seems that Being itself is likewise discharged and divested of all sovereignty. But the strongest objection against the principle of sovereignty is contained in Melville's Bartleby, the scrivener who, with his "I would prefer not to," resists every possibility of deciding between potentiality and the potentiality not to. These figures push the aporia of sovereignty to the limit but still do not completely free themselves from its ban. They show that the dissolution of the ban, like the cutting of the Gordian knot, resembles less the solution of a logical or mathematical problem than the solution of an enigma. Here the metaphysical aporia shows its political nature.

§ 4 Form of Law

4.1. In the legend "Before the Law," Kafka represented the structure of the sovereign ban in an exemplary abbreviation.

Nothing—and certainly not the refusal of the doorkeeper—prevents the man from the country from passing through the door of the Law if not the fact that this door is already open and that the Law prescribes nothing. The two most recent interpreters of the legend, Jacques Derrida and Massimo Cacciari, have both insisted on this point, if in different ways. "The Law," Derrida writes, "keeps itself [*se garde*] without keeping itself, kept [*gardée*] by a doorkeeper who keeps nothing, the door remaining open and open onto nothing" ("Préjugés," p. 356). And Cacciari, even more decisively, underlines the fact that the power of the Law lies precisely in the impossibility of entering into what is already open, of reaching the place where one already is: "How can we hope to 'open' if the door is already open? How can we hope to enter-the-open [*entrare-l'aperto*]? In the open, there is, things are there, one does not enter there. . . . We can enter only there where we can open. The already-open [*il già-aperto*] immobilizes. The man from the country cannot enter, because entering into what is already open is ontologically impossible" (*Icone*, p. 69).

Seen from this perspective, Kafka's legend presents the pure form in which law affirms itself with the greatest force precisely at the point in which it no longer prescribes anything—which is to say, as

49

pure ban. The man from the country is delivered over to the potentiality of law because law demands nothing of him and commands nothing other than its own openness. According to the schema of the sovereign exception, law applies to him in no longer applying, and holds him in its ban in abandoning him outside itself. The open door destined only for him includes him in excluding him and excludes him in including him. And this is precisely the summit and the root of every law. When the priest in *The Trial* summarizes the essence of the court in the formula "The court wants nothing from you. It receives you when you come, it lets you go when you go," it is the originary structure of the *nomos* that he states.

ℵ In an analogous fashion, language also holds man in its ban insofar as man, as a speaking being, has always already entered into language without noticing it. Everything that is presupposed for there to be language (in the forms of something nonlinguistic, something ineffable, etc.) is nothing other than a presupposition of language that is maintained as such in relation to language precisely insofar as it is excluded from language. Stéphane Mallarmé expressed this self-presuppositional nature of language when he wrote, with a Hegelian formula, "The logos is a principle that operates through the negation of every principle." As the pure form of relation, language (like the sovereign ban) always already presupposes itself in the figure of something nonrelational, and it is not possible either to enter into relation or to move out of relation with what belongs to the form of relation itself. This means not that the nonlinguistic is inaccessible to man but simply that man can never reach it in the form of a nonrelational and ineffable presupposition, since the nonlinguistic is only ever to be found in language itself. (In the words of Benjamin, only the "crystal-pure elimination of the unsayable in language" can lead to "what withholds itself from speech" [*Briefe*, p. 127].)

4.2. But does this interpretation of the structure of law truly exhaust Kafka's intention? In a letter to Benjamin dated September 20, 1934, Gerschom Scholem defines the relation to law described in Kafka's *Trial* as "the Nothing of Revelation" (*Nichts der Offenbarung*), intending this expression to name "a stage in which revelation does not signify [*bedeutet*], yet still affirms itself by the fact that it is in force. Where the wealth of significance is gone and what appears, reduced, so to speak, to the zero point of its own content, still does not disappear (and Revelation is something that appears), there the Nothing appears" (Benjamin and Scholem, *Briefwechsel*, p. 163). According to Scholem, a law that finds itself in such a condition is not absent but rather appears in the form of its unrealizability. "The students of whom you speak," he objects to his friend, "are not students who have lost the Scripture . . . but students who cannot decipher it" (ibid., p. 147).

Being in force without significance (*Geltung ohne Bedeutung*): nothing better describes the ban that our age cannot master than Scholem's formula for the status of law in Kafka's novel. What, after all, is the structure of the sovereign ban if not that of a law that *is in force* but does not *signify*? Everywhere on earth men live today in the ban of a law and a tradition that are maintained solely as the "zero point" of their own content, and that include men within them in the form of a pure relation of abandonment. All societies and all cultures today (it does not matter whether they are democratic or totalitarian, conservative or progressive) have entered into a legitimation crisis in which law (we mean by this term the entire text of tradition in its regulative form, whether the Jewish Torah or the Islamic Shariah, Christian dogma or the profane *nomos*) is in force as the pure "Nothing of Revelation." But this is precisely the structure of the sovereign relation, and the nihilism in which we are living is, from this perspective, nothing other than the coming to light of this relation as such.

4.3. In Kant the pure form of law as "being in force without significance" appears for the first time in modernity. What Kant calls "the simple form of law" (*die bloße Form des Gesetzes*) in the *Critique of Practical Reason* is in fact a law reduced to the zero point of its significance, which is, nevertheless, in force as such (*Kritik der praktischen Vernunft*, p. 28). "Now if we abstract every content, that is, every object of the will (as determining motive) from a law," he writes, "there is nothing left but the simple form of a universal legislation" (ibid., p. 27). A pure will, thus determined only through such a form of law, is "neither free nor unfree," exactly like Kafka's man from the country.

The limit and also the strength of the Kantian ethics lie precisely in having left the form of law in force as an empty principle. This being in force without significance in the sphere of ethics corresponds, in the sphere of knowledge, to the transcendental object. The transcendental object is, after all, not a real object but "merely the idea of relation" (*bloß eine Idee des Verhältnisses*) that simply expresses the fact of thinking's being in relation with an absolutely indeterminate thought (*Kants opus postuum*, p. 671).

But what is such a "form of law"? And how, first of all, is one to conduct oneself before such a "form of law," once the will is not determined by any particular content? What is the *form of life*, that is, that corresponds to the *form of law*? Does the moral law not become something like an "inscrutable faculty"? Kant gives the name "respect" (*Achtung*, reverential attention) to the condition of one who finds himself living under a law that is in force without signifying, and that thus neither prescribes nor forbids any determinate end: "The motivation that a man can have, before a certain end is proposed to him, clearly can be nothing other than the law itself through the respect that it inspires (without determining what goals it is possible to have or reach by obeying it). For once the content of free will is eliminated, the law is the only thing left in relation to the formal element of the free will" ("Über den Gemeinspruch," p. 282).

It is truly astounding how Kant, almost two centuries ago and under the heading of a sublime "moral feeling," was able to describe the very condition that was to become familiar to the mass societies and great totalitarian states of our time. For life under a law that is in force without signifying resembles life in the state of exception, in which the most innocent gesture or the smallest forgetfulness can have most extreme consequences. And it is exactly this kind of life that Kafka describes, in which law is all the more pervasive for its total lack of content, and in which a distracted knock on the door can mark the start of uncontrollable trials. Just as for Kant the purely formal character of the moral law founds its claim of universal practical applicability in every circumstance, so in Kafka's village the empty potentiality of law is so much in force as to become indistinguishable from life. The existence and the very body of Joseph K. ultimately coincide with the Trial; they *become* the Trial. Benjamin sees this clearly when he writes, objecting to Scholem's notion of a being in force without significance, that a law that has lost its content ceases to exist and becomes indistinguishable from life: "Whether the students have lost the Scripture or cannot decipher it in the end amounts to the same thing, since a Scripture without its keys is not Scripture but life, the life that is lived in the village at the foot of the hill on which the castle stands" (Benjamin and Scholem, *Briefwechsel,* p. 155). And this provokes Scholem (who does not notice that his friend has grasped the difference perfectly well) to insist that he cannot agree that "it is the same thing whether the students have lost their Scripture or cannot decipher it, and it even seems to me that this is the greatest mistake that can be made. I refer to precisely the difference between these two stages when I speak of a 'Nothing of Revelation'" (ibid., p. 163).

If, following our analyses, we see in the impossibility of distinguishing law from life—that is, in the life lived in the village at the foot of the castle—the essential character of the state of exception, then two different interpretations confront each other here: on the one hand, that of Scholem, which sees in this life the maintenance of the pure form of law beyond its own content—a being in force without significance—and, on the other hand, that of Benjamin, for which the state of exception turned into rule signals law's fulfillment and its becoming indistinguishable from the life over which it ought to rule. Confronted with the imperfect nihilism that would let the Nothing subsist indefinitely in the form of a being in force without significance, Benjamin proposes a messianic nihilism that nullifies even the Nothing and lets no form of law remain in force beyond its own content.

Whatever their exact meaning and whatever their pertinence to the interpretation of Kafka's text, it is certain that every inquiry into the relation between life and law today must confront these two positions.

א The experience of being in force without significance lies at the basis of a current of contemporary thought that is not irrelevant here. The prestige of deconstruction in our time lies precisely in its having conceived of the entire text of tradition as being in force without significance, a being in force whose strength lies essentially in its undecidability and in having shown that such a being in force is, like the door of the Law in Kafka's parable, absolutely impassable. But it is precisely concerning the sense of this being in force (and of the state of exception that it inaugurates) that our position distinguishes itself from that of deconstruction. Our age does indeed stand in front of language just as the man from the country in the parable stands in front of the door of the Law. What threatens thinking here is the possibility that thinking might find itself condemned to infinite negotiations with the doorkeeper or, even worse, that it might end by itself assuming the role of the doorkeeper who, without really blocking the entry, shelters the Nothing onto which the door opens. As the evangelical warning cited by Origen concerning the interpretation of Scripture has it: "Woe to you, men of the Law, for you have taken away the key to knowledge: you yourselves have not entered, and you have not let the others who approached enter either" (which ought to be reformulated as follows: "Woe to you, who have not wanted to enter into the door of the Law but have not permitted it to be closed either").

4.4. This is the context in which one must read both the singular "inversion" that Benjamin, in his essay on Kafka, opposes to law's being in force without significance, and the enigmatic allusion, in his eighth "Theses on the Philosophy of History," to a "real" state of exception. A life that resolves itself completely into writing corresponds, for Benjamin, to a Torah whose key has been lost: "I consider the sense of the inversion toward which many of Kafka's allegories tend to lie in an attempt to transform life into Scripture" (Benjamin and Scholem, *Briefwechsel,* p. 155). Analogously, the eighth thesis opposes a "real" (*wirklich*) state of exception, which it is our task to bring about, to the state of exception in which we live, which has become the rule: "The tradition of the oppressed teaches us that the 'state of exception' in which we live is the rule. We must arrive at a concept of history that corresponds to this fact. Then we will have the production of the real state of exception before us as a task" (Benjamin, "Über den Begriff," p. 697).

We have seen the sense in which law begins to coincide with life once it has become the pure form of law, law's mere being in force without significance. But insofar as law is maintained as pure form in a state of virtual exception, it lets bare life (K.'s life, or the life lived in the village at the foot of the castle) subsist before it. Law that becomes indistinguishable from life in a real state of exception is confronted by life that, in a symmetrical but inverse gesture, is entirely transformed into law. The absolute intelligibility of a life wholly resolved into writing corresponds to the impenetrability of a writing that, having become indecipherable, now appears as life. Only at this point do the two terms distinguished and kept united by the relation of ban (bare life and the form of law) abolish each other and enter into a new dimension.

4.5. Significantly, in the last analysis all the interpreters read the legend as the tale of the irremediable failure or defeat of the man from the country before the impossible task imposed upon him by the Law. Yet it is worth asking whether Kafka's text does not consent to a different reading. The interpreters seem to forget, in fact, precisely the words with which the story ends: "No one else could enter here, since this door was destined for you alone. Now I will go and shut it." If it is true the door's very openness constituted, as we saw, the invisible power and specific "force" of the Law, then we can imagine that all the behavior of the man from the country is nothing other than a complicated and patient strategy to have the door closed in order to interrupt the Law's being in force. And in the end, the man succeeds in his endeavor, since he succeeds in having the door of the Law closed forever (it was, after all, open "only for him"), even if he may have risked his life in the process (the story does not say that he is actually dead but only that he is "close to the end"). In his interpretation of the legend, Kurt

Weinberg has suggested that one must see the figure of a "thwarted Christian Messiah" in the shy but obstinate man from the country (*Kafkas Dichtungen*, pp. 130–31). The suggestion can be taken only if it is not forgotten that the Messiah is the figure in which the great monotheistic religions sought to master the problem of law, and that in Judaism, as in Christianity or Shiite Islam, the Messiah's arrival signifies the fulfillment and the complete consummation of the Law. In monotheism, messianism thus constitutes not simply one category of religious experience among others but rather the limit concept of religious experience in general, the point in which religious experience passes beyond itself and calls itself into question insofar as it is law (hence the messianic aporias concerning the Law that are expressed in both Paul's Epistle to the Romans and the Sabbatian doctrine according to which the fulfillment of the Torah is its transgression). But if this is true, then what must a messiah do if he finds himself, like the man from the country, before a law that is in force without signifying? He will certainly not be able to fulfill a law that is already in a state of suspension, nor simply substitute another law for it (the fulfillment of law is not a new law).

A miniature painting in a fifteenth-century Jewish manuscript containing Haggadoth on "He who comes" shows the arrival of the Messiah in Jerusalem. The Messiah appears on horseback (in other illustrations, the mount is a donkey) at the sacred city's wide-open gates, behind which a window shows a figure who could be a doorkeeper. A youth in front of the Messiah is standing one step from the open door and pointing toward it. Whoever this figure is (it might be the prophet Elijah), he can be likened to the man from the country in Kafka's parable. His task seems to be to prepare and facilitate the entry of the Messiah—a paradoxical task, since the door is wide open. If one gives the name "provocation" to the strategy that compels the potentiality of Law to translate itself into actuality, then his is a paradoxical form of provocation, the only form adequate to a law that is in force without signifying and a door that allows no one to enter on account of being too open. The messianic task of the man from the country (and of the youth who stands before the door in the miniature) might then be precisely that of making the virtual state of exception real, of compelling the doorkeeper to close the door of the Law (the door of Jerusalem). For the Messiah will be able to enter only after the door is closed, which is to say, after the Law's being in force without significance is at an end. This is the meaning of the enigmatic passage in Kafka's notebooks where he writes, "The Messiah will only come when he is no longer necessary, he will only come after his arrival, he will come not on the last day, but on the very last day." The final sense of the legend is thus not, as Derrida writes, that of an "event that succeeds in not happening" (or that happens in not happening: "an event that happens not to happen," *un événement qui arrive à ne pas arriver* ["Préjugés," p. 359]), but rather precisely the opposite: the story tells how something has really happened in seeming not to happen, and the messianic aporias of the man from the country express exactly the difficulties that our age must confront in attempting to master the sovereign ban.

א One of the paradoxes of the state of exception lies in the fact that in the state of exception, it is impossible to distinguish transgression of the law from execution of the law, such that what violates a rule and what conforms to it coincide without any remainder (a person who goes for a walk during the curfew is not transgressing the law any more than the soldier who kills him is executing it). This is precisely the situation that, in the Jewish tradition (and, actually, in every genuine messianic tradition), comes to pass when the Messiah arrives. The first consequence of this arrival is that the Law (according to the Kabbalists, this is the law of the Torah of Beriah, that is, the law in force from the creation of man until the messianic days) is fulfilled and consummated. But this fulfillment does not signify that the old law is simply replaced by a new law that is homologous to the old but has different prescriptions and different prohibitions (the Torah of Aziluth, the originary law that the Messiah, according to the Kabbalists, would restore, contains neither prescriptions nor prohibitions and is only a jumble of unordered letters). What is implied instead is that the fulfillment of the Torah now coincides with its transgression. This much is clearly affirmed by the most radical messianic movements, like that of Sabbatai Zevi (whose motto was "the fulfillment of the Torah is its transgression").

From the juridico-political perspective, messianism is therefore a theory of the state of exception—except for the fact that in messianism there is no authority in force to proclaim the state of exception; instead, there is the Messiah to subvert its power.

ℵ One of the peculiar characteristics of Kafka's allegories is that at their very end they offer the possibility of an about-face that completely upsets their meaning. The obstinacy of the man from the country thus suggests a certain analogy with the cleverness that allows Ulysses to survive the song of the Sirens. Just as the Law in "Before the Law" is insuperable because it prescribes nothing, so the most terrible weapon in Kafka's "The Sirens" is not song but silence ("it has never happened, but it might not be altogether unimaginable that someone could save himself from their song, but certainly never from their silence." Ulysses' almost super-human intelligence consists precisely in his having noticed that the Sirens were silent and in having opposed them with his trick "only as a shield," exactly as the man from the country does with respect to the doorkeeper of the Law. Like the "doors of India" in "The New Lawyer," the door of the Law can also be seen as a symbol of those mythic forces that man, like Bucephalus, the horse, must master at all costs.

4.6. Jean-Luc Nancy is the philosopher who has most rigorously reflected upon the experience of law that is implicit in this being in force without significance. In an extremely dense text, he identifies its ontological structure as that of abandonment and, consequently, attempts to conceive not only our time but the entire history of the West as the "time of abandonment." The structure he describes nevertheless remains inside the form of law, and abandonment is conceived as abandonment to the sovereign ban, without any way out of the ban being envisaged:

> To *abandon* is to remit, entrust, or turn over to . . . a sovereign power, and to remit, entrust, or turn over to its *ban*, that is, to its proclaiming, to its convening, and to its sentencing.
> One always abandons to a law. The destitution of abandoned Being is measured by the limitless severity of the law to which it finds itself exposed. Abandonment does not constitute a subpoena to present oneself before this or that court of law. It is a compulsion to appear absolutely under the law, under the law as such and in its totality. In the same way—it is the same thing—to be *banished* amounts not to

coming under a provision of the law but rather to coming under the entirety of the law. Turned over to the absolute of the law, the abandoned one is thereby abandoned completely outside its jurisdiction. . . . Abandonment respects the law; it cannot do otherwise. (*L'impératif catégorique*, pp. 149–50)

The task that our time imposes on thinking cannot simply consist in recognizing the extreme and insuperable form of law as being in force without significance. Every thought that limits itself to this does nothing other than repeat the ontological structure that we have defined as the paradox of sovereignty (or sovereign ban). Sovereignty is, after all, precisely this "law beyond the law to which we are abandoned," that is, the self-presuppositional power of *nomos*. Only if it is possible to think the Being of abandonment beyond every idea of law (even that of the empty form of law's being in force without significance) will we have moved out of the paradox of sovereignty toward a politics freed from every ban. A pure form of law is only the empty form of relation. Yet the empty form of relation is no longer a law but a zone of indistinguishability between law and life, which is to say, a state of exception.

Here the problem is the same one that Heidegger confronts in his *Beiträge zur Philosophie* under the heading of "Seinsverlassenheit," the abandonment of the entity by Being, which, in fact, constitutes nothing less than the problem of the unity and difference between Being and being in the age of the culmination of metaphysics. What is at issue in this abandonment is not something (Being) that dismisses and discharges something else (the being). On the contrary: *here Being is nothing other than the being's being abandoned and remitted to itself*; here Being is nothing other than the ban of the being:

What is abandoned by whom? The being by Being, which does and does not belong to it. The being then appears *thus*, it appears as object and as available Being, as if Being were not. . . . Then this is shown: that Being abandons the being means: Being dissimulates itself in the being-manifest of the being. And Being itself becomes essentially determined as this withdrawing self-dissimulation. . . . Abandoned by

Being: that Being abandons the being, that Being is consigned to itself and becomes the object of calculation. This is not simply a "fall" but the first history of Being itself. (*Beiträge zur Philosophie*, p. 115)

If Being in this sense is nothing other than Being *in the ban* of the being [*l'essere* a bandono *dell'ente*], then the ontological structure of sovereignty here fully reveals its paradox. The relation of abandonment is now to be thought in a new way. To read this relation as a being in force without significance—that is, as Being's abandonment *to* and *by* a law that prescribes nothing, and not even itself—is to remain inside nihilism and not to push the experience of abandonment to the extreme. Only where the experience of abandonment is freed from every idea of law and destiny (including the Kantian form of law and law's being in force without significance) is abandonment truly experienced as such. This is why it is necessary to remain open to the idea that the relation of abandonment is not a relation, and that *the being together of the being and Being does not have the form of relation*. This does not mean that Being and the being now part ways; instead, they remain without relation. But this implies nothing less than an attempt to think the politico-social *factum* no longer in the form of a relation.

ℵ Alexandre Kojève's idea of the end of history and the subsequent institution of a new homogenous state presents many analogies with the epochal situation we have described as law's being in force without significance (this explains the contemporary attempts to bring Kojève to life in a liberal-capitalist key). What, after all, is a State that survives history, a State sovereignty that maintains itself beyond the accomplishment of its *telos*, if not a law that is in force without signifying? To conceive of a fulfillment of history in which the empty form of sovereignty still persists is just as impossible as to conceive of an extinction of the State without the fulfillment of its historical forms, since the empty form of the State tends to generate epochal contents that, in turn, seek out a State form that has become impossible (this is what is happening in the ex–Soviet Union and in ex-Yugoslavia).

The only thought adequate to the task would be one capable of both thinking the end of the State and the end of history together and mobilizing the one against the other.

This is the direction in which the late Heidegger seems to move, if still insufficiently, with the idea of a final event or appropriation (*Ereignis*) in which what is appropriated is Being itself, that is, the principle that had until then determined beings in different epochs and historical figures. This means that with the *Ereignis* (as with the Hegelian Absolute in Kojève's reading), the "history of Being comes to an end" (Heidegger, *Zur Sache des Denkens*, p. 44), and the relation between Being and being consequently finds its "absolution." This is why Heidegger can write that with the *Ereignis* he is trying to think "Being without regard to the being," which amounts to nothing less than attempting to think the ontological difference no longer as a relation, and Being and being beyond every form of a connection.

This is the perspective from which we must situate the debate between Kojève and Georges Bataille. What is at play here is precisely the figure of sovereignty in the age of the fulfillment of human history. Various scenarios are possible. In the note added to the second edition of his *Introduction to the Reading of Hegel,* Kojève distances himself from the first edition's claim that the end of history simply coincides with man's becoming an animal again and the disappearance of man in the proper sense (that is, as the subject of negating action). During a trip to Japan in 1959, Kojève had maintained the possibility of a posthistorical culture in which men, while abandoning their negating action in the strict sense, continue to separate forms from their contents not in order to actively transform these contents but to practice a kind of "pure snobbism" (tea ceremonies, etc.). On the other hand, in the review of Raymond Queneau's novels he sees in the characters of *Dimanche de vie*, and particularly in the "lazy rascal" (*voyou desœuvré*), the figure of the satisfied wise man at the end of history (Kojève, "Les romans," p. 391). In opposition to the *voyou desœuvré* (who is contemptuously defined as *homo quenellenesis*) and the satisfied and self-conscious Hegelian wise man, Bataille proposes the figure of a sovereignty entirely consumed in the instant (*la seule innocence possible: celle de l'instant*) that coincides with "the forms in which man gives himself to himself: . . . laughter, eroticism, struggle, luxury."

The theme of *desœuvrement*—inoperativeness as the figure of the fullness of man at the end of history—which first appears in Kojève's review of Queneau, has been taken up by Blanchot and by Nancy, who places it at the very center of his work *The Inoperative Community.* Everything depends on what is meant by "inoperativeness." It can be neither the simple absence of work nor (as in Bataille) a sovereign and useless form of negativity. The only coherent way to understand inoperativeness is to think of it as a generic mode of potentiality that is not exhausted (like individual action or collective action understood as the sum of individual actions) in a *transitus de potentia ad actum.*

§ Threshold

In laying bare the irreducible link uniting violence and law, Benjamin's "Critique of Violence" proves the necessary and, even today, indispensable premise of every inquiry into sovereignty. In Benjamin's analysis, this link shows itself to be a dialectical oscillation between the violence that posits law and the violence that preserves it. Hence the necessity of a third figure to break the circular dialectic of these two forms of violence:

> The law of this oscillation [between the violence that posits law and the violence that preserves it] rests on the fact that all law-preserving violence, in its duration, indirectly weakens the lawmaking violence represented by it, through the suppression of hostile counterviolence. . . . This lasts until either new forces or those earlier suppressed triumph over the violence that had posited law until now and thus found a new law destined to a new decay. In the interruption of this cycle, which is maintained by mythical forms of law, in the deposition of law and all the forces on which it depends (as they depend on it) and, therefore, finally in the deposition of State power, a new historical epoch is founded. ("Zur Kritik der Gewalt," p. 202)

The definition of this third figure, which Benjamin calls "divine violence," constitutes the central problem of every interpretation of the essay. Benjamin in fact offers no positive criterion for its identification and even denies the possibility of recognizing it in the concrete case. What is certain is only that it neither posits nor preserves law, but rather "de-poses" (*entsetzt*) it. Hence its capacity to lend itself to the most dangerous equivocations (which is proven by the scrutiny with which Derrida, in his interpretation of the essay, guards against it, approximating it—with a peculiar misunderstanding—to the Nazi "Final Solution" ["Force of Law," pp. 1044–45]).

It is likely that in 1920, at the time Benjamin was working on the "Critique," he had not yet read Schmitt's *Political Theology*, whose definition of sovereignty he would cite five years later in his book on the Baroque mourning play. Sovereign violence and the state of exception, therefore, do not appear in the essay, and it is not easy to say where they would stand with respect to the violence that posits law and the violence that preserves it. The root of the ambiguity of divine violence is perhaps to be sought in precisely this absence. The violence exercised in the state of exception clearly neither preserves nor simply posits law, but rather conserves it in suspending it and posits it in excepting itself from it. In this sense, sovereign violence, like divine violence, cannot be wholly reduced to either one of the two forms of violence whose dialectic the essay undertook to define. This does not mean that sovereign violence can be confused with divine violence. The definition of divine violence becomes easier, in fact, precisely when it is put in relation with the state of exception. Sovereign violence opens a zone of indistinction between law and nature, outside and inside, violence and law. And yet the sovereign is precisely the one who maintains the possibility of deciding on the two to the very degree that he renders them indistinguishable from each other. As long as the state of exception is distinguished from the normal case, the dialectic between the violence that posits law and the violence that preserves it is not truly broken, and the sovereign decision even appears simply as the medium in which the passage from the one to the other takes place. (In this sense, it can be said both that sovereign violence posits law, since it affirms that an otherwise forbidden act is permitted, and that it conserves law, since the content of the new law is only the conservation of the old one.) In any case, the link between violence and law is maintained, even at the point of their indistinction.

The violence that Benjamin defines as divine is instead situated in a zone in which it is no longer possible to distinguish between exception and rule. It stands in the same relation to sovereign violence as the state of actual exception, in the eighth thesis, does to the state of virtual exception. This is why (that is, insofar as divine violence is not one kind of violence among others but only the dissolution of the link between violence and law) Benjamin can say that divine violence neither posits nor conserves violence, but deposes it. Divine violence shows the connection between the two violences—and, even more, between violence and law—to be the single real content of law. "The function of violence in juridical creation," Benjamin writes, at the only point in which the essay approaches something like a definition of sovereign violence, "is twofold, in the sense that lawmaking pursues as its end, with violence as the means, what is to be established as law, but at the moment of its instatement does not depose violence; rather, at this very moment of lawmaking and in the name of power, it specifi-cally establishes as law not an end immune and independent from violence, but one necessarily and intimately bound up with it" ("Zur Kritik der Gewalt," pp. 197–98). This is why it is not by chance that Benjamin, with a seemingly abrupt development, concentrates on the bearer of the link between violence and law, which he calls "bare life" (*bloßes Leben*), instead of defining divine violence. The analysis of this figure—whose decisive function in the economy of the essay has until now remained unthought—establishes an essential link between bare life and juridical violence. Not only does the rule of law over the living exist and cease to exist alongside bare life, but even the dissolution of juridical violence, which is in a certain sense the object of the essay, "stems . . . from the guilt of bare natural life, which consigns the living, innocent and unhappy, to the punishment that 'expiates' the guilt of bare life—and doubtless also purifies [*entsühnt*] the guilty, not of guilt, however, but of law" (ibid., p. 200).

In the pages that follow, we will attempt to develop these suggestions and to analyze the link binding bare life to sovereign power. According to Benjamin, the principle of the sacred character of life, which our age assigns to human life and even to animal life, can be of no use either in clarifying this link or in calling into question the rule of law over the living. To Benjamin, it is suspicious that what is here proclaimed as sacred is precisely what, according to mythical thought, is "the bearer destined to guilt: bare life," almost as if there were a secret complicity between the sacredness of life and the power of law. "It might," he writes, "be well worth while to investigate the origin of the dogma of the sacredness of life. Perhaps, indeed probably, it is relatively recent, the last mistaken attempt of the weakened Western tradition to seek the saint it had lost in cosmological impenetrability" (ibid., p. 202).

We shall begin by investigating precisely this origin. The principle of the sacredness of life has become so familiar to us that we seem to forget that classical Greece, to which we owe most of our ethico-political concepts, not only ignored this principle but did not even possess a term to express the complex semantic sphere that we indicate with the single term "life." Decisive as it is for the origin of Western politics, the opposition between *zoē* and *bios*, between *zēn* and *eu zēn* (that is, between life in general and the qualified way of life proper to men), contains nothing to make one assign a privilege or a sacredness to life as such. Homeric Greek does not even know a term to designate the living body. The term *sōma*, which appears in later epochs as a good equivalent to our term "life," originally meant only "corpse," almost as if life in itself, which for the Greeks was broken down into a plurality of forms and elements, appeared only as a unity after death. Moreover, even in those societies that, like classical Greece, celebrated animal sacrifices and occasionally immolated human victims, life in itself was not considered sacred. Life became sacred only through a series of rituals whose aim was precisely to separate life from its profane context. In the words of Benveniste, to render the victim sacred, it is necessary to "separate it from the world of the living, it is necessary that it cross the threshold that separates the two universes: this is the aim of the killing" (*Le vocabulaire*, p. 188).

If this is true, then when and in what way did a human life first come to be considered sacred in itself? Until now we have been concerned with delineating the logical and topological structure of sovereignty. But what is excepted and captured in sovereignty, and who is the bearer of the sovereign ban? Both Benjamin and Schmitt, if differently, point to life ("bare life" in Benjamin and, in Schmitt, the "real life" that "breaks the crust of a mechanism rigidified through repetition") as the element that, in the exception, finds itself in the most intimate relation with sovereignty. It is this relation that we must now clarify.

PART TWO

Homo Sacer

§ 1 Homo Sacer

1.1. Pompeius Festus, in his treatise *On the Significance of Words*, under the heading *sacer mons* preserved the memory of a figure of archaic Roman law in which the character of sacredness is tied for the first time to a human life as such. After defining the Sacred Mount that the plebeians consecrated to Jove at the time of their secession, Festus adds:

> At homo sacer is est, quem populus iudicavit ob maleficium; neque fas est eum immolari, sed qui occidit, parricidi non damnatur; nam lege tribunicia prima cavetur "si quis eum, qui eo plebei scito sacer sit, occiderit, parricidia ne sit." Ex quo quivis homo malus atque improbus sacer appellari solet. (*De verborum significatione*)

> The sacred man is the one whom the people have judged on account of a crime. It is not permitted to sacrifice this man, yet he who kills him will not be condemned for homicide; in the first tribunitian law, in fact, it is noted that "if someone kills the one who is sacred according to the plebiscite, it will not be considered homicide." This is why it is customary for a bad or impure man to be called sacred.

The meaning of this enigmatic figure has been much discussed, and some have wanted to see in it "the oldest punishment of Roman criminal law" (Bennett, "Sacer esto," p. 5). Yet every interpretation of *homo sacer* is complicated by virtue of having to concentrate on traits that seem, at first glance, to be contradictory.

71

In an essay of 1930, H. Bennett already observes that Festus's definition "seems to deny the very thing implicit in the term" (ibid., p. 7), since while it confirms the sacredness of a person, it authorizes (or, more precisely, renders unpunishable) his killing (whatever etymology one accepts for the term *parricidium*, it originally indicated the killing of a free man). The contradiction is even more pronounced when one considers that the person whom anyone could kill with impunity was nevertheless not to be put to death according to ritual practices (*neque fas est eum immolari*: *immolari* indicates the act of sprinkling the *mola salsa* on the victim before killing him).

In what, then, does the sacredness of the sacred man consist? And what does the expression *sacer esto* ("May he be sacred"), which often figures in the royal laws and which already appears in the archaic inscription on the forum's rectangular *cippus*, mean, if it implies at once the *impune occidi* ("being killed with impunity") and an exclusion from sacrifice? That this expression was also obscure to the Romans is proven beyond the shadow of a doubt by a passage in Ambrosius Theodosius Macrobius's *Saturnalia* (3.7.3–8) in which the author, having defined *sacrum* as what is destined to the gods, adds: "At this point it does not seem out of place to consider the status of those men whom the law declares to be sacred to certain divinities, for I am not unaware that it appears strange [*mirum videri*] to some people that while it is forbidden to violate any sacred thing whatsoever, it is permitted to kill the sacred man." Whatever the value of the interpretation that Macrobius felt obliged to offer at this point, it is certain that sacredness appeared problematic enough to him to merit an explanation.

1.2. The perplexity of the *antiqui auctores* is matched by the divergent interpretations of modern scholars. Here the field is divided between two positions. On the one hand, there are those, like Theodor Mommsen, Ludwig Lange, Bennett, and James Leigh Strachan-Davidson, who see *sacratio* as a weakened and secularized residue of an archaic phase in which religious law was not yet distinguished from penal law and the death sentence appeared as a sacrifice to the gods. On the other hand, there are those, like Károly Kerényi and W. Ward Fowler, who consider *sacratio* to bear the traces of an archetypal figure of the sacred—consecration to the gods of the underworld—which is analogous to the ethnological notion of taboo: august and damned, worthy of veneration and provoking horror. Those among the first group are able to admit the *impune occidi* (as, for example, Mommsen does in terms of a popular or vicariate execution of a death sentence), but they are still unable to explain the ban on sacrifice. Inversely, the *neque fas est eum immolari* is understandable in the perspective of the second group of scholars ("*homo sacer*," Kerényi writes, "cannot be the object of sacrifice, of a *sacrificium*, for no other reason than this very simple one: what is *sacer* is already possessed by the gods and is originarily and in a special way possessed by the gods of the underworld, and so there is no need for it to become so through a new action" [*La religione*, p. 76]). But it remains completely incomprehensible from this perspective why anyone can kill *homo sacer* without being stained by sacrilege (hence the incongruous explanation of Macrobius, according to which since the souls of the *homines sacri* were *diis debitae*, they were sent to the heavens as quickly as possible).

Neither position can account economically and simultaneously for the two traits whose juxtaposition, according to Festus, constitutes the specificity of *homo sacer*: *the unpunishability of his killing and the ban on his sacrifice*. In the light of what we know of the Roman juridical and religious order (both of the *ius divinum* and the *ius humanum*), the two traits seem hardly compatible: if *homo sacer* was impure (Fowler: *taboo*) or the property of the gods (Kerényi), then why could anyone kill him without either contaminating himself or committing sacrilege? What is more, if *homo sacer* was truly the victim of a death sentence or an archaic sacrifice, why is it not *fas* to put him to death in the prescribed forms of execution? What, then, is the life of *homo sacer*, if it is situated at the intersection of a capacity to be killed and yet not sacrificed, outside both human and divine law?

It appears that we are confronted with a limit concept of the

Roman social order that, as such, cannot be explained in a satisfying manner as long as we remain inside either the *ius divinum* or the *ius humanum*. And yet *homo sacer* may perhaps allow us to shed light on the reciprocal limits of these two juridical realms. Instead of appealing to the ethnological notion of taboo in order to dissolve the specificity of *homo sacer* into an assumed originary ambiguity of the sacred—as has all too often been done—we will try to interpret *sacratio* as an autonomous figure, and we will ask if this figure may allow us to uncover an originary *political* structure that is located in a zone prior to the distinction between sacred and profane, religious and juridical. To approach this zone, however, it will first be necessary to clear away a certain misunderstanding.

§ 2 The Ambivalence of the Sacred

2.1. Interpretations of social phenomena and, in particular, of the origin of sovereignty, are still heavily weighed down by a scientific mythologeme that, constituted between the end of the nineteenth century and the first decades of the twentieth, has consistently led the social sciences astray in a particularly sensitive region. This mythologeme, which we may provisionally call "the theory of the ambivalence of the sacred," initially took form in late Victorian anthropology and was immediately passed on to French sociology. Yet its influence over time and its transmission to other disciplines have been so tenacious that, in addition to compromising Bataille's inquiries into sovereignty, it is present even in that masterpiece of twentieth-century linguistics, Émile Benveniste's *Indo-European Language and Society*. It will not seem surprising that this mythologeme was first formulated in William Robertson Smith's *Lectures on the Religion of the Semites* (1889)—the same book that was to influence the composition of Freud's *Totem and Taboo* ("reading it," Freud wrote, "was like slipping away on a gondola")—if one keeps in mind that these *Lectures* correspond to the moment in which a society that had already lost every connection to its religious tradition began to express its own unease. In Smith's book, the ethnographic notion of taboo first leaves the sphere of primitive cultures and firmly penetrates the study of biblical religion, thereby irrevocably marking the Western experience of the sacred with its ambiguity. "Thus," Smith writes in the fourth lecture,

> alongside of taboos that exactly correspond to rules of holiness, pro-
> tecting the inviolability of idols and sanctuaries, priests and chiefs, and
> generally of all persons and things pertaining to the gods and their
> worship, we find another kind of taboo which in the Semitic field has
> its parallel in rules of uncleanness. Women after child-birth, men who
> have touched a dead body and so forth are temporarily taboo and
> separated from human society, just as the same persons are unclean in
> Semitic religion. In these cases the person under taboo is not regarded
> as holy, for he is separated from approach to the sanctuary as well as
> from contact with men. . . . In most savage societies no sharp line
> seems to be drawn between the two kinds of taboo just indicated, and
> even in more advanced nations the notions of holiness and unclean-
> ness often touch. (Smith, *Lectures*, pp. 152–53)

In a note added to the second edition of his *Lectures*, under the title "Holiness, Uncleanness and Taboo," Smith lists a new series of examples of ambiguity (among which is the ban on pork, which "in the most elevated Semitic religions appears as a kind of no-man's-land between the impure and the sacred") and postulates the impossibility of "separating the Semitic doctrine of the holy from the impurity of the taboo-system" (ibid., p. 452).

It is significant that Smith also mentions the ban in his list of examples of this ambiguous power (*patens*) of the sacred:

> Another Hebrew usage that may be noted here is the ban (Heb.
> *ḥerem*), by which impious sinners, or enemies of the community and
> its god, were devoted to utter destruction. The ban is a form of
> devotion to the deity, and so the verb "to ban" is sometimes rendered
> "consecrate" (Micah 4: 13) or "devote" (Lev. 27: 28ff.). But in the oldest
> Hebrew times it involved the utter destruction, not only of the persons
> involved, but of their property . . . and only metals, after they had
> passed through the fire, were added to the treasure of the sanctuary
> (Josh. 6: 24). Even cattle were not sacrificed, but simply slain, and the
> devoted city must not be revealed (Deut. 13: 6; Josh. 6: 26). Such a ban
> is a taboo, enforced by the fear of supernatural penalties (1 Kings 16:

34), and, as with taboo, the danger arising from it is contagious (Deut. 7: 26); he that brings a devoted thing into his house falls under the same ban itself. (*Lectures*, pp. 453–54)

The analysis of the ban—which is assimilated to the taboo—determines from the very beginning the genesis of the doctrine of the ambiguity of the sacred: the ambiguity of the ban, which excludes in including, implies the ambiguity of the sacred.

2.2. Once it is formulated, the theory of the ambivalence of the sacred has no difficulty extending itself over every field of the social sciences, as if European culture were only now noticing it for the first time. Ten years after the *Lectures*, the classic of French anthropology, Marcel Mauss and H. Hubert's "Essay on the Nature and Function of Sacrifice" (1889) opens with an evocation of precisely "the ambiguous character of sacred things, which Robertson Smith has so admirably made clear" ("Essai," p. 195). Six years later, in the second volume of Wilhelm Max Wundt's *Völkerpsychologie*, the concept of taboo would express precisely the originary indistinction of sacred and impure that is said to characterize the most archaic period of human history, constituting that mixture of veneration and horror described by Wundt—with a formula that was to enjoy great success—as "sacred horror." According to Wundt, it was therefore only in a later period, when the most ancient powers were replaced by the gods, that the originary ambivalence gave way to the opposition of the sacred and the impure.

In 1912, Mauss's uncle, Émile Durkheim, published his *Elementary Forms of Religious Life*, in which an entire chapter is devoted to "the ambiguity of the notion of the sacred." Here he classifies the "religious forces" as two opposite categories, the auspicious and the inauspicious:

To be sure, the sentiments provoked by the one and the other are not identical: disgust and horror are one thing and respect another. Nonetheless, for actions to be the same in both cases, the feelings expressed must not be different in kind. In fact, there actually is a certain horror in religious respect, especially when it is very intense; and the fear inspired by malignant powers is not without a certain reverential quality. . . . The pure and the impure are therefore not two separate genera, but rather two varieties of the same genus that includes sacred things. There are two kinds of sacred things, the auspicious and the inauspicious. Not only is there no clear border between these two opposite kinds, but the same object can pass from one to the other without changing nature. The impure is made from the pure, and vice versa. The ambiguity of the sacred consists in the possibility of this transmutation. (*Les formes élémentaires*, pp. 446–48)

What is at work here is the psychologization of religious experience (the "disgust" and "horror" by which the cultured European bourgeoisie betrays its own unease before the religious fact), which will find its final form in Rudolph Otto's work on the sacred. Here, in a concept of the sacred that completely coincides with the concept of the obscure and the impenetrable, a theology that had lost all experience of the revealed word celebrated its union with a philosophy that had abandoned all sobriety in the face of feeling. That the religious belongs entirely to the sphere of psychological emotion, that it essentially has to do with shivers and goose bumps— this is the triviality that the neologism "numinous" had to dress up as science.

When Freud set out to write *Totem and Taboo* several years later, the field had therefore already been prepared for him. Yet only with this book does a genuine general theory of the ambivalence of the sacred come to light on the basis not only of anthropology and psychology but also of linguistics. In 1910, Freud had read the essay "On the Antithetical Meaning of Primal Words" by the now discredited linguist Karl Abel, and he reviewed it for *Imago* in an article in which he linked Abel's essay to his own theory of the absence of the principle of contradiction in dreams. The Latin term *sacer*, "sacred and damned," figures in the list of words with antithetical meanings that Abel gives in his appendix, as Freud does not hesitate to point out. Strangely enough, the anthropologists who first formulated the theory of the ambiguity of the sacred did not mention the Latin concept of *sacratio*. But in 1911, Fowler's essay "The Original Meaning of the Word *Sacer*" appeared, presenting an interpretation of *homo sacer* that had an immediate effect on the scholars of religious studies. Here the implicit ambiguity in Festus's definition allows the scholar (taking up a suggestion of Robert Marett's) to link the Latin *sacer* with the category of taboo: "*Sacer esto* is in fact a curse; and *homo sacer* on whom this curse falls is an outcast, a banned man, tabooed, dangerous. . . . Originally the word may have meant simply taboo, i.e. removed out of the region of the *profanum*, without any special reference to a deity, but 'holy' or accursed according to the circumstances" (Fowler, *Roman Essays*, pp. 17–23).

In a well-documented study, Huguette Fugier has shown how the doctrine of the ambiguity of the sacred penetrates into the sphere of linguistics and ends by having its stronghold there (*Recherches*, pp. 238–40). A decisive role in this process is played precisely by *homo sacer*. While in the second edition of A. Walde's *Lateinisches etymologisches Wörterbuch* (1910) there is no trace of the doctrine of the ambivalence of the sacred, the entry under the heading *sacer* in Alfred Ernout-Meillet's *Dictionnaire étymologique de la langue latine* (1932) confirms the "double meaning" of the term by reference to precisely *homo sacer*: "*Sacer* designates the person or the thing that one cannot touch without dirtying oneself or without dirtying; hence the double meaning of 'sacred' or 'accursed' (approximately). A guilty person whom one consecrates to the gods of the underworld is sacred (*sacer esto*: cf. Grk. *agios*)."

ℵ It is interesting to follow the exchanges documented in Fugier's work between anthropology, linguistics, and sociology concerning the problem of the sacred. Pauly-Wilson's "Sacer" article, which is signed by R. Ganschinietz (1920) and explicitly notes Durkheim's theory of ambivalence (as Fowler had already done for Smith), appeared between the second edition of Walde's *Wörterbuch* and the first edition of Ernout-Meillet's *Dictionnaire*. As for Ernout-Meillet, Fugier notes the strict links that linguistics had with the Parisian school of sociology (in particular with Mauss and Durkheim). When Roger Callois published *Man and the Sacred* in 1939, he was thus able to start off directly with a lexical given, which was by then considered certain: "We know, following Ernout-Meillet's definition, that in Rome the word *sacer* designated the person or the thing that one cannot touch without dirtying oneself or without dirtying" (*L'homme et le sacré*, p. 22).

2.3. An enigmatic archaic Roman legal figure that seems to embody contradictory traits and therefore had to be explained thus begins to resonate with the religious category of the sacred when this category irrevocably loses its significance and comes to assume contradictory meanings. Once placed in relation with the ethnographic concept of taboo, this ambivalence is then used—with perfect circularity—to explain the figure of *homo sacer*. There is a moment in the life of concepts when they lose their immediate intelligibility and can then, like all empty terms, be overburdened with contradictory meanings. For the religious phenomenon, this moment coincides with the point at which anthropology—for which the ambivalent terms *mana, taboo*, and *sacer* are absolutely central—was born at the end of the last century. Lévi-Strauss has shown how the term *mana* functions as an excessive signifier with no meaning other than that of marking an excess of the signifying function over all signifieds. Somewhat analogous remarks could be made with reference to the use and function of the concepts of the sacred and the taboo in the discourse of the social sciences between 1890 and 1940. An assumed ambivalence of the generic religious category of the sacred cannot explain the juridico-political phenomenon to which the most ancient meaning of the term *sacer* refers. On the contrary, only an attentive and unprejudiced delimitation of the respective fields of the political and the religious will make it possible to understand the history of their intersection and complex relations. It is important, in any case, that the originary juridico-political dimension that presents itself in *homo sacer* not be covered over by a scientific mythologeme that not only explains nothing but is itself in need of explanation.

§ 3 Sacred Life

3.1. According to both the original sources and the consensus of scholars, the structure of *sacratio* arises out of the conjunction of two traits: the unpunishability of killing and the exclusion from sacrifice. Above all, the *impune occidi* takes the form of an exception from the *ius humanum* insofar as it suspends the application of the law on homicide attributed to Numa Pompilius: *Si quis hominem liberum dolo sciens morti duit, parricidas esto*, "If someone intentionally kills a free man, may he be considered a murderer." The very formulation given by Festus in some way even constitutes a real *exceptio* in the technical sense, which the killer, invoking the sacredness of the victim, could have opposed to the prosecution in the case of a trial. If one looks closely, however, one sees that even the *neque fas est eum immolari* ("it is not licit to sacrifice him") takes the form of an exception, this time from the *ius divinum* and from every form of ritual killing. The most ancient recorded forms of capital punishment (the terrible *poena cullei*, in which the condemned man, with his head covered in a wolf-skin, was put in a sack with serpents, a dog and a rooster, and then thrown into water, or defenestration from the Tarpean rock) are actually purification rites and not death penalties in the modern sense: the *neque fas est eum immolari* served precisely to distinguish the killing of *homo sacer* from ritual purifications, and decisively excluded *sacratio* from the religious sphere in the strict sense.

It has been observed that while *consecratio* normally brings an object from the *ius humanum* to the *ius divinum,* from the profane to the sacred (Fowler, *Roman Essays,* p. 18), in the case of *homo sacer* a person is simply set outside human jurisdiction without being brought into the realm of divine law. Not only does the ban on immolation exclude every equivalence between the *homo sacer* and a consecrated victim, but—as Macrobius, citing Trebatius, observes—the fact that the killing was permitted implied that the violence done to *homo sacer* did not constitute sacrilege, as in the case of the *res sacrae* (*Cum cetera sacra violari nefas sit, hominem sacrum ius fuerit occidi,* "While it is forbidden to violate the other sacred things, it is licit to kill the sacred man").

If this is true, then *sacratio* takes the form of a double exception, both from the *ius humanum* and from the *ius divinum,* both from the sphere of the profane and from that of the religious. The topological structure drawn by this double exception is that of a double exclusion and a double capture, which presents more than a mere analogy with the structure of the sovereign exception. (Hence the pertinence of the view of those scholars who, like Giuliano Crifò, interpret *sacratio* in substantial continuity with the exclusion from the community [Crifò, "Exilica causa," pp. 460–65].) Just as the law, in the sovereign exception, applies to the exceptional case in no longer applying and in withdrawing from it, so *homo sacer* belongs to God in the form of unsacrificeability and is included in the community in the form of being able to be killed. *Life that cannot be sacrificed and yet may be killed is sacred life.*

3.2. What defines the status of *homo sacer* is therefore not the originary ambivalence of the sacredness that is assumed to belong to him, but rather both the particular character of the double exclusion into which he is taken and the violence to which he finds himself exposed. This violence—the unsanctionable killing that, in his case, anyone may commit—is classifiable neither as sacrifice nor as homicide, neither as the execution of a condemnation to death nor as sacrilege. Subtracting itself from the sanctioned forms of both human and divine law, this violence opens a sphere of human action that is neither the sphere of *sacrum facere* nor that of profane action. This sphere is precisely what we are trying to understand here.

We have already encountered a limit sphere of human action that is only ever maintained in a relation of exception. This sphere is that of the sovereign decision, which suspends law in the state of exception and thus implicates bare life within it. We must therefore ask ourselves if the structure of sovereignty and the structure of *sacratio* might be connected, and if they might, from this perspective, be shown to illuminate each other. We may even then advance a hypothesis: once brought back to his proper place beyond both penal law and sacrifice, *homo sacer* presents the originary figure of life taken into the sovereign ban and preserves the memory of the originary exclusion through which the political dimension was first constituted. The political sphere of sovereignty was thus constituted through a double exclusion, as an excrescence of the profane in the religious and of the religious in the profane, which takes the form of a zone of indistinction between sacrifice and homicide. *The sovereign sphere is the sphere in which it is permitted to kill without committing homicide and without celebrating a sacrifice, and sacred life—that is, life that may be killed but not sacrificed—is the life that has been captured in this sphere.*

It is therefore possible to give a first answer to the question we put to ourselves when we delineated the formal structure of the exception. What is captured in the sovereign ban is a human victim who may be killed but not sacrificed: *homo sacer*. If we give the name bare life or sacred life to the life that constitutes the first content of sovereign power, then we may also arrive at an answer to the Benjaminian query concerning "the origin of the dogma of the sacredness of life." The life caught in the sovereign ban is the life that is originarily sacred—that is, that may be killed but not sacrificed—and, in this sense, the production of bare life is the originary activity of sovereignty. The sacredness of life, which is invoked today as an absolutely fundamental right in opposition to sovereign power, in fact originally expresses precisely both life's subjection to a power over death and life's irreparable exposure in the relation of abandonment.

א The *potestas sacrosancta* that lay within the competence of the plebeian courts in Rome also attests to the link between *sacratio* and the constitution of a political power. The inviolability of the court is founded on the mere fact that when the plebeians first seceded, they swore to avenge the offenses committed against their representative by considering the guilty man a *homo sacer*. The Latin term *lex sacrata*, which improperly designated (the plebeians were originally clearly distinct from the *leges*) what was actually only a *charté jurée* (Magdelain, *La loi*, p. 57) of the insurrectionary plebs, originally had no other meaning than that of determining a life that can be killed. Yet for this very reason, the *lex sacrata* founded a political power that in some way counterbalanced the sovereign power. This is why nothing shows the end of the old republican constitution and the birth of the new absolute power as clearly as the moment in which Augustus assumed the *potestas tribunicia* and thus becomes *sacrosanctus*. (*Sacrosanctus in perpetuum ut essem*, the text of *Res gestae* declares, *et quoad viverem tribunicia potestas mihi tribuetur*, "So that I may be forever sacrosanct, and that the tribunitian power may be attributed to me for my whole life.")

3.3. Here the structural analogy between the sovereign exception and *sacratio* shows its full sense. At the two extreme limits of the order, the sovereign and *homo sacer* present two symmetrical figures that have the same structure and are correlative: the sovereign is the one with respect to whom all men are potentially *homines sacri*, and *homo sacer* is the one with respect to whom all men act as sovereigns.

The sovereign and *homo sacer* are joined in the figure of an action that, excepting itself from both human and divine law, from both *nomos* and *physis*, nevertheless delimits what is, in a certain sense, the first properly political space of the West distinct from both the religious and the profane sphere, from both the natural order and the regular juridical order.

This symmetry between *sacratio* and sovereignty sheds new light on the category of the sacred, whose ambivalence has so tenaciously oriented not only modern studies on the phenomenology of religion but also the most recent inquiries into sovereignty. The proximity between the sphere of sovereignty and the sphere of the sacred, which has often been observed and explained in a variety of ways, is not simply the secularized residue of the originary religious character of every political power, nor merely the attempt to grant the latter a theological foundation. And this proximity is just as little the consequence of the "sacred"—that is, august and accursed—character that inexplicably belongs to life as such. If our hypothesis is correct, sacredness is instead the originary form of the inclusion of bare life in the juridical order, and the syntagm *homo sacer* names something like the originary "political" relation, which is to say, bare life insofar as it operates in an inclusive exclusion as the referent of the sovereign decision. Life is sacred only insofar as it is taken into the sovereign exception, and to have exchanged a juridico-political phenomenon (*homo sacer*'s capacity to be killed but not sacrificed) for a genuinely religious phenomenon is the root of the equivocations that have marked studies both of the sacred and of sovereignty in our time. *Sacer esto* is not the formula of a religious curse sanctioning the *unheimlich*, or the simultaneously august and vile character of a thing: it is instead the originary political formulation of the imposition of the sovereign bond.

The crimes that, according to the original sources, merit *sacratio* (such as *terminum exarare*, the cancellation of borders; *verberatio parentis*, the violence of the son against the parent; or the swindling of a client by a counsel) do not, therefore, have the character of a transgression of a rule that is then followed by the appropriate sanction. They constitute instead the originary exception in which human life is included in the political order in being exposed to an unconditional capacity to be killed. Not the act of tracing boundaries, but their cancellation or negation is the constitutive act of the city (and this is what the myth of the foundation of Rome, after all, teaches with perfect clarity). Numa's homicide law (*parricidas esto*) forms a system with *homo sacer*'s capacity to be killed (*parricidi non damnatur*) and cannot be separated from it. The originary structure by which sovereign power is founded is this complex.

‫‪ℵ‬‬ Consider the sphere of meaning of the term *sacer* as it appears in our analysis. It contains neither an antithetical meaning in Abel's sense nor a generic ambivalence in Durkheim's sense. It indicates, rather, a life that may be killed by anyone—an object of a violence that exceeds the sphere both of law and of sacrifice. This double excess opens the zone of indistinction between and beyond the profane and the religious that we have attempted to define. From this perspective, many of the apparent contradictions of the term "sacred" dissolve. Thus the Latins called pigs *pure* if they were held to be fit for sacrifice ten days after their birth. But Varro (*De re rustica,* 2. 4. 16) relates that in ancient times the pigs fit for sacrifice were called *sacres.* Far from contradicting the unsacrificeability of *homo sacer,* here the term gestures toward an originary zone of indistinction in which *sacer* simply meant a life that could be killed. (Before the sacrifice, the piglet was not yet "sacred" in the sense of "consecrated to the gods," but only capable of being killed.) When the Latin poets define lovers as *sacred* (*sacros qui ledat amantes,* "whoever harms the sacred lovers" [Propertius, 3. 6. 2]; *Quisque amore teneatur, eat tutusque sacerque,* "May whoever is in love be safe and sacred" [Tibullus, 1. 2. 27]), this is not because they are accursed or consecrated to the gods but because they have separated themselves from other men in a sphere beyond both divine and human law. Originally, this sphere was the one produced by the double exception in which sacred life was exposed.

§ 4 'Vitae Necisque Potestas'

4.1. "For a long time, one of the characteristic privileges of sovereign power was the right to decide life and death." Foucault's statement at the end of the first volume of the *History of Sexuality* (*La volonté*, p. 119) sounds perfectly trivial. Yet the first time we encounter the expression "right over life and death" in the history of law is in the formula *vitae necisque potestas*, which designates not sovereign power but rather the unconditional authority [*potestà*] of the *pater* over his sons. In Roman law, *vita* is not a juridical concept but instead indicates either the simple fact of living or a particular way of life, as in ordinary Latin usage (in a single term, Latin brings together the meaning of both *zoē* and *bios*). The only place in which the word *vita* acquires a specifically juridical sense and is transformed into a real *terminus technicus* is in the very expression *vitae necisque potestas*. In an exemplary study, Yan Thomas has shown that *que* in this formula does not have a disjunctive function and that *vita* is nothing but a corollary of *nex*, the power to kill ("Vita," pp. 508–9). Life thus originally appears in Roman law merely as the counterpart of a power threatening death (more precisely, death without the shedding of blood, since this is the proper meaning of *necare* as opposed to *mactare*). This power is absolute and is understood to be neither the sanction of a crime nor the expression of the more general power that lies within the competence of the *pater* insofar as he is the head of the *domus*: this

87

power follows immediately and solely from the father-son relation (in the instant in which the father recognizes the son in raising him from the ground, he acquires the power of life and death over him). And this is why the father's power should not be confused with the power to kill, which lies within the competence of the father or the husband who catches his wife or daughter in the act of adultery, or even less with the power of the *dominus* over his servants. While both of these powers concern the domestic jurisdiction of the head of the family and therefore remain, in some way, within the sphere of the *domus*, the *vitae necisque potestas* attaches itself to every free male citizen from birth and thus seems to define the very model of political power in general. *Not simple natural life, but life exposed to death (bare life or sacred life) is the originary political element.*

The Romans actually felt there to be such an essential affinity between the father's *vitae necisque potestas* and the magistrate's *imperium* that the registries of the *ius patrium* and of the sovereign power end by being tightly intertwined. The theme of the *pater imporiosus* who himself bears both the character of the father and the capacity of the magistrate and who, like Brutus or Manlius Torquatus, does not hesitate to put the treacherous son to death, thus plays an important role in the anecdotes and mythology of power. But the inverse figure of the father who exerts his *vitae necisque potestas* over his magistrate son, as in the case of the consul Spurius Cassius and the tribune Caius Flaminius, is just as decisive. Referring to the story of the latter, who was dragged down from the rostra by his father while he was trying to supersede the authority of the senate, Valerius Maximus defines the father's *potestas*, significantly, as an *imperium privatum*. Thomas, who has analyzed these episodes, could write that in Rome the *patria potestas* was felt to be a kind of public duty and to be, in some way, a "residual and irreducible sovereignty" ("Vita," p. 528). And when we read in a late source that in having his sons put to death, Brutus "had adopted the Roman people in their place," it is the same power of death that is now transferred, through the image of adoption, to the entire people. The hagiographic epithet "father of the people," which is reserved in every age to the leaders invested with sovereign authority, thus once again acquires its originary, sinister meaning. What the source presents us with is therefore a kind of genealogical myth of sovereign power: the magistrate's *imperium* is nothing but the father's *vitae necisque potestas* extended to all citizens. There is no clearer way to say that the first foundation of political life is a life that may be killed, which is politicized through its very capacity to be killed.

4.2. From this perspective, it is possible to see the sense of the ancient Roman custom according to which only the prepubescent son could place himself between the magistrate equipped with the *imperium* and the lictor who went before him. The physical proximity of the magistrate to the lictors who always accompanied him bearing the terrible insignias of power (the *fasces formidulosi* and the *saeve secures*) firmly expresses the inseparability of the *imperium* from a power of death. If the son can place himself between the magistrate and the lictor, it is because he is already originarily and immediately subject to a power of life and death with respect to the father. The *puer* son symbolically affirms precisely the consubstantiality of the *vitae necisque potestas* with sovereign power.

At the point in which the two seem to coincide, what emerges is the singular fact (which by now should not appear so singular) that every male citizen (who can as such participate in public life) immediately finds himself in a state of virtually being able to be killed, and is in some way *sacer* with respect to his father. The Romans were perfectly aware of the aporetic character of this power, which, flagrantly contradicting the principle of the Twelve Tables according to which a citizen could not be put to death without trial (*indemnatus*), took the form of a kind of unlimited authorization to kill (*lex indemnatorum interficiendum*). Moreover, the other characteristic that defines the exceptionality of sacred life—the impossibility of being put to death according to sanctioned ritual practices—is also to be found in the *vitae necisque potestas*. Thomas refers ("Vita," p. 540) to the case recalled as a rhetorical exercise by Calpurnius Flaccus, in which a father, by virtue of his *potestas*, gives his son over to an executioner to be killed. The son resists and rightly demands that his father be the one to put him to death (*vult manu patris interfici*). The *vitae necisque potestas* immediately attaches itself to the bare life of the son, and the *impune occidi* that derives from it can in no way be assimilated to the ritual killing following a death sentence.

4.3. At a certain point, Thomas poses a question concerning the *vitae necisque potestas*: "What is this incomparable bond for which Roman law is unable to find any expression other than death?" ("Vita," p. 510). The only possible answer is that what is at issue in this "incomparable bond" is the inclusion of bare life in the juridico-political order. It is as if male citizens had to pay for their participation in political life with an unconditional subjection to a power of death, as if life were able to enter the city only in the double exception of being capable of being killed and yet not sacrificed. Hence the situation of the *patria potestas* at the limit of both the *domus* and the city: if classical politics is born through the separation of these two spheres, life that may be killed but not sacrificed is the hinge on which each sphere is articulated and the threshold at which the two spheres are joined in becoming indeterminate. Neither political *bios* nor natural *zoē*, sacred life is the zone of indistinction in which *zoē* and *bios* constitute each other in including and excluding each other.

It has been rightly observed that the state is founded not as the expression of a social tie but as an untying (*déliaison*) that prohibits (Badiou, *L'être*, p. 125). We may now give a further sense to this claim. *Déliaison* is not to be understood as the untying of a preexisting tie (which would probably have the form of a pact or a contract). The tie itself originarily has the form of an untying or exception in which what is captured is at the same time excluded, and in which human life is politicized only through an abandonment to an unconditional power of death. The sovereign tie is more originary than the tie of the positive rule or the tie of the social pact, but the sovereign tie is in truth only an untying. And what this untying implies and produces—bare life, which dwells in the no-man's-land between the home and the city—is, from the point of view of sovereignty, the originary political element.

§ 5 Sovereign Body and Sacred Body

5.1. When Ernst Kantorowicz published *The King's Two Bodies: A Study in Mediaeval Political Theology* in the United States at the end of the 1950s, the book was received with great favor not only by medievalists but also and above all by historians of the modern age and scholars of political science and the theory of the state. The work was without doubt a masterpiece of its kind, and the notion that it advanced of a "mystical" or "political body" of the sovereign certainly constituted (as Kantorowicz's most brilliant pupil, R. E. Giesey, observed years later) a "milestone in the history of the development of the modern state" (Giesey, *Cérémonial,* p. 9). Such unanimous favor in such a delicate area ought, however, to provoke some reflection.

In his preface, Kantorowicz himself notes that the book, which was born as an inquiry into the medieval precedents of the juridical doctrine of the king's two bodies, had gone beyond the author's first intention and had even transformed itself—as the subtitle indicates —into a "study in mediaeval political theology." Kantorowicz, who had lived through and intensely participated in the political affairs of Germany in the 1920s, fighting alongside the Nationalists in the Spartacist Revolt in Berlin and the Republic of Councils in Munich, could not have failed to intend the reference to the "political theology" under whose insignia Schmitt had placed his own theory of sovereignty in 1922. Thirty-five years later, after Nazism had marked an irreparable rupture in his life as an assimilated Jew, Kantorowicz returned to interrogate, from a completely different perspective, the "Myth of the State" that he had ardently shared in his youth. In a significant disavowal, the preface warns: "It would go much too far . . . to assume that the author felt tempted to investigate the emergence of some of the idols of modern political religions merely on account of the horrifying experience of our own time in which whole nations, the largest and the smallest, fell prey to the weirdest dogmas and in which political theologisms became genuine obsessions" (*King's Two Bodies*, p. viii). And with the same eloquent modesty, the author writes that he "cannot claim to have demonstrated in any completeness the problem of what has been called 'The Myth of the State'" (ibid., p. ix).

In this sense it has been possible to read the book, not without reason, as one of our century's great critical texts on the state and techniques of power. Yet anyone who has followed the patient work of analysis that leads from the macabre irony of *Richard II* and Plowden's reports to a reconstruction of the formation of the doctrine of the king's two bodies in medieval jurisprudence and theology cannot fail to wonder if the book really can indeed be read as only a demystification of political theology. The fact of the matter is that while the political theology evoked by Schmitt essentially frames a study of the absolute character of political power, *The King's Two Bodies* is instead exclusively concerned with the other, more innocuous feature that, according to Jean Bodin, defines sovereignty (*puissance absolue et perpétuelle*)—the perpetual nature of sovereignty, which allows the royal *dignitas* to survive the physical person of its bearer (*Le roi ne meurt jamais*, "The king never dies"). Here "Christian political theology" was, by means of analogy with Christ's mystic body, directed solely toward the task of establishing the continuity of the state's *corpus morale et politicum* (moral and political body), without which no stable political organization could be conceived. And it is in this sense that "notwithstanding . . . some similarities with disconnected pagan concepts, the king's two bodies is an offshoot of Christian theological thought and, consequently, stands as a landmark of Christian political theology" (*King's Two Bodies*, p. 434).

5.2. Advancing this final thesis decisively, Kantorowicz evokes— but immediately sets aside—precisely the element that could have steered the genealogy of the doctrine of the king's two bodies in a less reassuring direction. Kantorowicz connects the doctrine of the king's two bodies with the other, darker mystery of sovereign power: *la puissance absolue*. In chapter 7, describing the peculiar funeral ceremonies of French kings in which a wax effigy of the sovereign, placed on a *lit d'honneur*, occupied an important position and was fully treated as the king's living person, Kantorowicz suggests that these ceremonies might well have their origin in the apotheosis of Roman emperors. Here too, after the sovereign dies, his wax *imago*, "treated like a sick man, lies on a bed; senators and matrons are lined up on either side; physicians pretend to feel the pulse of the image and give it their medical aid until, after seven days, the effigy 'dies' " (*King's Two Bodies*, p. 427). According to Kantorowicz, however, the pagan precedent, while very similar, had not directly influenced the French ceremony. It was in any case certain to Kantorowicz that the presence of the effigy was to be once again placed in relation to the perpetuity of royal dignity, which "never dies."

That Kantorowicz's exclusion of the Roman precedent was not a product of negligence or oversight is shown by the attention which Giesey, with his teacher's full approval, gives to the matter in a book that can be considered a fitting completion of *The King's Two Bodies*, namely, *The Royal Funeral Ceremony in Renaissance France* (1960). Giesey could not ignore the fact that a genetic connection between imperial Roman *consecratio* and the French rite had been established by such scholars as Elias Bickermann and the very eminent Julius Schlosser. Curiously enough, Giesey nevertheless suspends judgment on the matter ("as far as I am concerned," he writes, "I prefer not to choose either of the two solutions" [p. 128]) and instead resolutely confirms his teacher's interpretation of the link between the effigy and the perpetual character of sovereignty. There was an obvious reason for this choice: if the hypothesis of the pagan derivation of the image ceremony had been taken into account, the Kantorowiczian thesis concerning "Christian political theology" would have fallen by the wayside or would, at least, have had to be reformulated more cautiously. But there was a different—and more secret—reason, and that is that nothing in Roman *consecratio* allowed one to place the emperor's effigy in relation to what is sovereignty's clearest feature, its perpetual nature. The macabre and grotesque rite in which an image was first treated as a living person and then solemnly burned gestured instead toward a darker and more uncertain zone, which we will now investigate, in which the political body of the king seemed to approximate—and even to become indistinguishable from—the body of *homo sacer*, which can be killed but not sacrificed.

5.3. In 1929, a young scholar of classical antiquity, Elias Bicker-mann, published an article titled "Roman Imperial Apotheosis" in the *Archiv für Religionswissenschaft*, which, in a short but detailed appendix, explicitly placed the pagan image ceremony (*funus imaginarium*) in relation to the funeral rites of English and French sovereigns. Both Kantorowicz and Giesey cite this study; Giesey even declares, without hesitation, that his own work originated in a reading of Bickermann's article. Both Kantorowicz and Giesey remain silent, however, about what was precisely the central point of Bickermann's analysis.

Carefully reconstructing the rite of imperial consecration from both written sources and coins, Bickermann had discerned the specific aporia contained in this "funeral by image," even if he had not grasped all of its consequences:

> Every normal man is buried only once, just as he dies only once. In the age of Antonius, however, the consecrated emperor is burned on the funeral pyre twice, first *in corpore* and then *in effigie*. . . . The emperor's corpse is solemnly, but not officially, burned, and his remains are deposited in the mausoleum. At this point public mourning usually

ends. . . . But in Antonius Pius's funeral, everything is carried out contrary to usual practice. Here *Iustitium* (public mourning) begins only after the burial of the bones, and the state funeral procession starts up once the remains of the corpse already lie buried in the ground! And this *funus publicum*, as we learn from Dio's and Herodian's reports of later consecrations, concerns the wax effigy made after the image of the deceased sovereign. . . . Dio reports as an eyewitness that a slave uses a fan to keep flies away from the face of the doll. Then Septimus Severus gives him a farewell kiss on the funeral pyre. Herodian adds that the image of Septimus Severus is treated in the palace as a sick person for seven days, with doctors' visits, clinical reports, and diagnoses of death. All of these accounts leave no doubt: the wax effigy, which is "in all things similar" to the dead man, and which lies on the official bed wearing the dead man's clothes, is the emperor himself, whose life has been transferred to the wax doll by means of this and perhaps other magical rites. ("Die römische Kaiserapotheose," pp. 4–6)

Yet what is decisive for understanding the whole ritual is precisely the function and the nature of the image. Here Bickermann suggests a comparison that makes it possible to situate the ceremony in a new perspective:

Parallels for such picture magic are numerous and can be found all over the world. Here it suffices to cite an Italic example from the year 136. A quarter of a century before the funeral of the effigy of Antonius Pius, the *lex collegii culorum Dianae et Antinonoi* declares: *Quisquis ex hoc collegio servus defunctus fuerit et corpus eius a domino iniquo sepulturae datum non . . . fuerit . . . , ei funus imaginarium fiet* [If a servant of this college dies and an impious master does not bury the body, may a *funus imaginarium* be performed]. Here we find the same expression, *funus imaginarium*, that the "Historia Augusta" uses to designate the funeral ceremony of Pertinax's wax effigy at which Dio was present. In the *lex collegii* as in other parallel cases, however, the image functions as a substitute for the missing corpse; in the case of the imperial ceremony, it appears instead beside the corpse, doubling the dead body without substituting for it. (ibid., pp. 6–7)

In 1972, returning to the problem after more than 40 years, Bickermann places the imaginary imperial funeral in relation to a rite required for the warrior who, after having solemnly dedicated himself to the Manes gods before fighting, does not die in battle (*Consecratio*, p. 22). And it is here that the body of the sovereign and the body of *homo sacer* enter into a zone of indistinction in which they can no longer be told apart.

5.4. For a long time now, scholars have approximated the figure of *homo sacer* to that of the *devotus* who consecrates his own life to the gods of the underworld in order to save the city from a grave danger. Livy has left us a vivid, meticulous description of a *devotio* that took place in 340 B.C.E. during the battle of Veseris. The Roman army was about to be defeated by its Latin adversaries when the consul Publius Decius Mus, who was commanding the legions alongside his colleague Titus Manlius Torquatus, asked the pontifex to assist him in carrying out the rite:

> The pontiff ordered him to put on the purple-bordered toga and, with his head veiled and one hand thrust out from the toga and touching his chin, to stand on a spear that was laid under his feet, and to say as follows: "Janus, Jupiter, Father Mars, Quirinus, Bellona, Lares, divine Novensiles, divine Indigites, you gods in whose power are both we and our enemies, and you, divine Manes—I invoke and worship you, I beseech and crave your favor, that you prosper the might and victory of the Roman People of the Quirites, and visit the foes of the Roman People of the Quirites with fear, shuddering, and death. As I have pronounced these words, even so in behalf of the republic of the Roman People of the Quirites, and of the army, the legions, the auxiliaries of the Roman People of the Quirites, do I consign and consecrate [*devoveo*] the legions and auxiliaries of the enemy, together with myself, to the divine Manes and to Earth. . . ." Then, having girded himself with the Gabinian cincture, he rose up armed on his horse and plunged into the thick of the enemy. To both armies he appeared more august than a man, as though sent from heaven to expiate the anger of the gods. (Livy, *Ab urbe condita libri*, 8. 9. 4ff.)

Here the analogy between *devotus* and *homo sacer* does not seem to go beyond the fact that both are in some way consecrated to death and belong to the gods, even if (despite Livy's parallel) not in the technical form of sacrifice. Yet Livy contemplates a hypothesis that sheds significant light on this institution and makes it possible to assimilate the life of the *devotus* more strictly to that of *homo sacer*:

> It seems proper to add here that the consul, dictator, or praetor who consecrates the legions of the enemy not only can consecrate himself but can also consecrate any citizen whatsoever who belongs to a Roman legion. If the man who has been consecrated dies, it is deemed that all is well; but if he does not die, then an image [*signum*] of him must be buried seven feet or more under the ground and a victim must be immolated in expiation. And no Roman magistrate may walk over the ground in which the image has been buried. But if he has consecrated himself, as Decius did, and if he does not die, he cannot perform any rite, either public or private. (ibid., 8. 9. 13)

Why does the survival of the devotee constitute such an embarrassing situation for the community that it forces it to perform a complex ritual whose sense is so unclear? What is the status of the living body that seems no longer to belong to the world of the living? In an exemplary study, Robert Schilling observes that if the surviving devotee is excluded from both the profane world and the sacred world, "this happens because this man is *sacer*. He cannot be given back in any way to the profane world because it is precisely thanks to his consecration that the entire community was able to be spared the wrath of the gods" ("Sacrum et profanum," p. 956). This is the perspective from which we must see the statue that we have already encountered in the emperor's *funus imaginarium* and that seems to unite, in one constellation, the body of the sovereign and the body of the devotee.

We know that the seven-foot-tall *signum* of which Livy speaks is none other than the devotee's "colossus," which is to say, his double, which takes the place of the missing corpse in a kind of funeral *per imaginem* or, more precisely, in the vicarious execution of an unfulfilled consecration. Jean-Pierre Vernant and Émile Benveniste have shown the general function of the colossus: this figure, attracting and establishing within itself a double in unusual conditions, "makes it possible to reestablish correct relations between the world of the living and the world of the dead" (Vernant, *Mythe*, p. 77). The first consequence of death is the liberation of a vague and threatening being (the *larva* of the Latins, the *psychē*, *eidōlon* or *phasma* of the Greeks) who returns, with the outward appearance of the dead person, to the places where the person lived, belonging properly neither to the world of the living nor to that of the dead. The goal of the funeral rites is to assure that this uncomfortable and uncertain being is transformed into a friendly and powerful ancestor, who clearly belongs to the world of the dead and with whom it is possible to maintain properly ritual relations. The absence of the corpse (or, in certain cases, its mutilation) can, however, impede the orderly fulfillment of the funeral rite. And in these cases a colossus can, under determinate conditions, be substituted for the corpse, thereby rendering possible a vicarious execution of the funeral.

What happens to the surviving devotee? Here it is not possible to speak of a missing corpse in the strict sense, for there has not even been a death. An inscription found in Cyrene nevertheless tells us that a colossus could even be made during the lifetime of the person for whom it was meant to substitute. The inscription bears the text of an oath that settlers leaving for Africa and the citizens of the homeland had to swear at Thera in order to secure their obligations to each other. At the moment they swore the oath, they threw wax *kolossoi* into a fire, saying, "May he who is unfaithful to this oath, as well as all his descendants and all his goods, be liquefied and disappear" (Vernant, *Mythe*, p. 69). The colossus is not, therefore, a simple substitute for the corpse. In the complex system regulating the relation between the living and the dead in the classical world, the colossus represents instead—analogously to the corpse, but in a more immediate and general way—that part of the person that is consecrated to death and that, insofar as it occupies the threshold between the two worlds, must be separated from the normal context of the living. This separation usually happens at the time of death, through the funeral rites that reestablish the proper relation between the living and the dead that had been disturbed by the deceased. In certain cases, however, it is not death that disturbs this order but rather its absence, and the fabrication of the colossus is then necessary to reestablish order.

Until this rite (which, as H. S. Versnel has shown, is not a vicarious funeral but rather a substitutive performance of a consecration ["Self-Sacrifice," p. 157]) is performed, the surviving devotee is a paradoxical being, who, while seeming to lead a normal life, in fact exists on a threshold that belongs neither to the world of the living nor to the world of the dead: he is a living dead man, or a living man who is actually a *larva*, and the colossus represents the very consecrated life that was, at the moment of the ritual by which he became a *devotus*, virtually separated from him.

5.5. If we now examine the life of *homo sacer* from this perspective, it is possible to assimilate his status to that of a surviving devotee for whom neither vicarious expiation nor substitution by a colossus is possible. The very body of *homo sacer* is, in its capacity to be killed but not sacrificed, a living pledge to his subjection to a power of death. And yet this pledge is, nevertheless, absolute and unconditional, and not the fulfillment of a consecration. It is therefore not by chance that in a text that has long appeared to interpreters to be confused and corrupt (*Saturnalia*, 3. 7. 6), Macrobius assimilates *homo sacer* to the statues (*Zanes*) in Greece that were consecrated to Jove with the proceeds from the fees imposed on oath-breaking athletes, statues that were in fact nothing other than the *collossi* of those who had broken their word and had therefore been vicariously consigned to divine justice (*animas . . . sacratorum hominum, quos zanas Graeci vocant,* "souls of the sacred men whom the Greeks call *Zanes*"). Insofar as he incarnates in his own person the elements that are usually distinguished from death, *homo sacer* is, so to speak, a living statue, the double or the colossus of himself. In the body of the surviving devotee and, even more unconditionally, in the body of *homo sacer*, the ancient world finds itself confronted for the first time with a life that, excepting itself in a double exclusion from the real context of both the profane and the religious forms of life, is defined solely by virtue of having

entered into an intimate symbiosis with death without, nevertheless, belonging to the world of the deceased. In the figure of this
"sacred life," something like a bare life makes its appearance in the
Western world. What is decisive, however, is that from the beginning this sacred life has an eminently political character and exhibits an essential link with the terrain on which sovereign power is
founded.

5.6. We must examine in this light the rite of the image in the
Roman imperial apotheosis. If the colossus always represents a life
consecrated to death in the sense we have seen, this means that the
death of the emperor (despite the presence of the corpse, whose
remains are ritually buried) frees a supplement of sacred life that, as
in the case of the man who has survived consecration, must be
neutralized by means of a colossus. Thus it is as if the emperor had
in himself not two bodies but rather two lives inside one single
body: a natural life and a sacred life. The latter, regardless of the
regular funeral rite, survives the former and can only ascend to the
heavens and be deified after the *funus imaginarium*. What unites
the surviving devotee, *homo sacer*, and the sovereign in one single
paradigm is that in each case we find ourselves confronted with a
bare life that has been separated from its context and that, so to
speak surviving its death, is for this very reason incompatible with
the human world. In every case, sacred life cannot dwell in the city
of men: for the surviving devotee, the imaginary funeral functions
as a vicarious fulfillment of the consecration that gives the individual back to normal life; for the emperor, the double funeral makes
it possible to fasten onto the sacred life, which must be gathered
and divinized in the apotheosis; for *homo sacer*, finally, we are
confronted with a residual and irreducible bare life, which must be
excluded and exposed to a death that no rite and no sacrifice can
redeem.

   In all three cases, sacred life is in some way tied to a political
function. It is as if, by means of a striking symmetry, supreme
power—which, as we have seen, is always *vitae necisque potestas* and
always founded on a life that may be killed but not sacrificed—

required that the very person of sovereign authority assume within itself the life held in its power. And if, for the surviving devotee, a missing death liberates this sacred life, for the sovereign, death reveals the excess that seems to be as such inherent in supreme power, as if supreme power were, in the last analysis, nothing other than *the capacity to constitute oneself and others as life that may be killed but not sacrificed.*

With respect to the interpretation of Kantorowicz and Giesey, the doctrine of the king's two bodies therefore appears in a different and less innocuous light. If this doctrine's relation to pagan imperial consecration cannot be bracketed, the very meaning of the theory changes radically. The king's political body (which, as Plowden says, "cannot be seen or touched" and which, "lacking childhood and old age and all the other defects to which the natural body is subject," exalts the mortal body to which it is joined) is, in the last analysis, derived from the emperor's colossus. Yet for this very reason, the king's political body cannot simply represent (as Kantorowicz and Giesey held) the continuity of sovereign power. The king's body must also and above all represent the very excess of the emperor's sacred life, which is isolated in the image and then, in the Roman ritual, carried to the heavens, or, in the French and English rite, passed on to the designated successor. However, once this is acknowledged, the metaphor of the political body appears no longer as the symbol of the perpetuity of *dignitas*, but rather as the cipher of the absolute and inhuman character of sovereignty. The formulas *le mort saisit le vif* and *le roi ne meurt jamais* must be understood in a much more literal way than is usually thought: at the moment of the sovereign's death, it is the sacred life grounding sovereign authority that invests the person of the sovereign's successor. The two formulas only signify sovereign power's continuity to the extent that they express, by means of the hidden tie to life that can be killed but not sacrificed, sovereign power's absoluteness.

For this reason, when Bodin, the most perceptive modern theorist of sovereignty, considers the maxim cited by Kantorowicz as an expression of the perpetuity of political power, he interprets it with reference to the absoluteness of political power: "This is why," he writes in the sixth book of *The Commonweale*, "it is said in this kingdom that the king never dies. And this saying, which is an ancient proverb, well shows that the kingdom was never elective, and that it has its scepter not from the Pope, nor from the Archbishop of Rheims, nor from the people, but rather from God alone" (*La République*, p. 985).

5.7. If the symmetry we have tried to illustrate between the body of the sovereign and that of *homo sacer* is correct, then we ought to be able to find analogies and correspondences in the juridico-political status of these two apparently distant bodies. Material for a first and immediate comparison is offered by the sanction that the killing of the sovereign incurs. We know that the killing of *homo sacer* does not constitute homicide (*parricidi non damnatur*). Accordingly, there is no juridico-political order (even among those societies in which homicide is always punished with capital punishment) in which the killing of the sovereign is classified simply as an act of homicide. Instead it constitutes a special crime, which is defined (once the notion of *maiestas*, starting with Augustus, is associated more and more closely with the person of the emperor) as *crimen lesae maiestatis*. It does not matter, from our perspective, that the killing of *homo sacer* can be considered as less than homicide, and the killing of the sovereign as more than homicide; what is essential is that in neither case does the killing of a man constitute an offense of homicide. When we still read in King Charles Albert of Savoy's statute that "the person of the sovereign is sacred and inviolable," we must hear, in the adjectives invoked, an echo of the sacredness of *homo sacer*'s life, which can be killed by anyone without committing homicide.

Yet the other defining characteristic of *homo sacer*'s life, that is, his unsacrificeability according to the forms prescribed by the rite of the law, is also to be found in the person of the sovereign. Michael Walzer has observed that in the eyes of the people of the time, the enormity of the rupture marked by Louis XVI's decapitation on January 21, 1793, consisted not in the fact that a monarch was killed but in the fact that he was submitted to a trial and executed after having been condemned to capital punishment ("King's Trial," pp. 184–85). In modern constitutions, a trace of the unsacrificeability of the sovereign's life still survives in the principle according to which the head of state cannot be submitted to an ordinary legal trial. In the American Constitution, for example, impeachment requires a special session of the Senate presided over by the chief justice, which can be convened only for "high crimes and misdemeanors," and whose consequence can never be a legal sentence but only dismissal from office. When the Jacobins suggested, during the discussions of the 1792 convention, that the king be executed without trial, they merely brought the principle of the unsacrificeability of sacred life to the most extreme point of its development, remaining absolutely faithful (though most likely they did not realize it) to the *arcanum* according to which sacred life may be killed by anyone without committing homicide, but never submitted to sanctioned forms of execution.

§ 6 The Ban and the Wolf

6.1. "The entire character of *homo sacer* shows that it was not born on the soil of a constituted juridical order, but goes all the way back to the period of pre-social life. It is a fragment of the primitive life of Indo-European peoples. . . . In the bandit and the outlaw (*wargus, vargr,* the wolf and, in the religious sense, the sacred wolf, *vargr y veum*), Germanic and Scandinavian antiquity give us a brother of *homo sacer* beyond the shadow of any doubt. . . . That which is considered to be an impossibility for Roman antiquity— the killing of the proscribed outside a judge and law—was an incontestable reality in Germanic antiquity" (Jhering, *L'esprit du droit romain,* p. 282).

Rodolphe Jhering was, with these words, the first to approximate the figure of *homo sacer* to that of the *wargus,* the wolf-man, and of the *Friedlos,* the "man without peace" of ancient Germanic law. He thus placed *sacratio* in the context of the doctrine of *Friedlosigkeit* that Wilhelm Eduard Wilda had elaborated toward the middle of the nineteenth century, according to which ancient Germanic law was founded on the concept of peace (*Fried*) and the corresponding exclusion from the community of the wrongdoer, who therefore became *friedlos,* without peace, and whom anyone was permitted to kill without committing homicide. The medieval ban also presents analogous traits: the bandit could be killed (*bannire idem est quod dicere quilibet possit eum offendere,* " 'To ban' someone is to say that anyone may harm him" [Cavalca, *Il bando*, p. 42]) or was even considered to be already dead (*exbannitus ad mortem de sua civitate debet haberi pro mortuo*, "Whoever is banned from his city on pain of death must be considered as dead" [ibid., p. 50]). Germanic and Anglo-Saxon sources underline the bandit's liminal status by defining him as a wolf-man (*wargus, werwolf,* the Latin *garulphus,* from which the French *loup garou,* "werewolf," is derived): thus Salic law and Ripuarian law use the formula *wargus sit, hoc est expulsus* in a sense that recalls the *sacer esto* that sanctioned the sacred man's capacity to be killed, and the laws of Edward the Confessor (1030–35) define the bandit as a *wulfesheud* (a wolf's head) and assimilate him to the werewolf (*lupinum enim gerit caput a die utlagationis suae, quod ab anglis wulfesheud vocatur,* "He bears a wolf's head from the day of his expulsion, and the English call this *wulfesheud*"). What had to remain in the collective unconscious as a monstrous hybrid of human and animal, divided between the forest and the city—the werewolf—is, therefore, in its origin the figure of the man who has been banned from the city. That such a man is defined as a wolf-man and not simply as a wolf (the expression *caput lupinum* has the form of a juridical statute) is decisive here. The life of the bandit, like that of the sacred man, is not a piece of animal nature without any relation to law and the city. It is, rather, a threshold of indistinction and of passage between animal and man, *physis* and *nomos,* exclusion and inclusion: the life of the bandit is the life of the *loup garou,* the werewolf, who is precisely *neither man nor beast,* and who dwells paradoxically within both while belonging to neither.

6.2. Only in this light does the Hobbesian mythologeme of the state of nature acquire its true sense. We have seen that the state of nature is not a real epoch chronologically prior to the foundation of the City but a principle internal to the City, which appears at the moment the City is considered *tanquam dissoluta,* "as if it were dissolved" (in this sense, therefore, the state of nature is something like a state of exception). Accordingly, when Hobbes founds sovereignty by means of a reference to the state in which "man is a wolf

to men," *homo hominis lupus,* in the word "wolf" (*lupus*) we ought
to hear an echo of the *wargus* and the *caput lupinem* of the laws of
Edward the Confessor: at issue is not simply *fera bestia* and natural
life but rather a zone of indistinction between the human and the
animal, a werewolf, a man who is transformed into a wolf and a
wolf who is transformed into a man—in other words, a bandit, a
homo sacer. Far from being a prejuridical condition that is indifferent to the law of the city, the Hobbesian state of nature is the
exception and the threshold that constitutes and dwells within it. It
is not so much a war of all against all as, more precisely, a condition
in which everyone is bare life and a *homo sacer* for everyone else,
and in which everyone is thus *wargus, gerit caput lupinum.* And this
lupization of man and humanization of the wolf is at every moment possible in the *dissolutio civitatis* inaugurated by the state of
exception. This threshold alone, which is neither simple natural
life nor social life but rather bare life or sacred life, is the always
present and always operative presupposition of sovereignty.

Contrary to our modern habit of representing the political realm
in terms of citizens' rights, free will, and social contracts, from the
point of view of sovereignty *only bare life is authentically political.*
This is why in Hobbes, the foundation of sovereign power is to be
sought not in the subjects' free renunciation of their natural right
but in the sovereign's preservation of his natural right to do anything to anyone, which now appears as the right to punish. "This is
the foundation," Hobbes states, "of that right of Punishing, which
is exercised in every Common-wealth. For the Subjects did not give
the Soveraign that right; but onely in laying down theirs, strength-
ned him to use his own, as he should think fit, for the preservation
of them all: so that it was not *given,* but *left* to him, and to him
onely; and (excepting the limits set him by naturall Law) as entire,
as in the condition of meer Nature, and of warre of every one
against his neighbour" (*Leviathan,* p. 214, emphasis added).

Corresponding to this particular status of the "right of Punishing," which takes the form of a survival of the state of nature at the
very heart of the state, is the subjects' capacity not to disobey but to
resist violence exercised on their own person, "for . . . no man is

supposed bound by Covenant, not to resist violence; and consequently it cannot be intended, that he gave any right to another to lay violent hands upon his person" (ibid.). Sovereign violence is in truth founded not on a pact but on the exclusive inclusion of bare life in the state. And just as sovereign power's first and immediate referent is, in this sense, the life that may be killed but not sacrificed, and that has its paradigm in *homo sacer*, so in the person of the sovereign, the werewolf, the wolf-man of man, dwells permanently in the city.

‫‬ In *Bisclavret*, one of Marie de France's most beautiful lays, both the werewolf's particular nature as the threshold of passage between nature and politics, animal world and human world, and the werewolf's close tie to sovereign power are presented with extraordinary vividness. The lay tells of a baron who is particularly close to his king (*de sun seinur esteit privez* [v. 19]), but who, every week, after hiding his clothes under a stone, is transformed into a werewolf (*bisclavret*) for three days, during which time he lives in the woods stealing and preying on other creatures (*al plus espés de la gaudine/s'i vif de preie e de ravine*). His wife, who suspects something, induces him to confess his secret life and convinces him to reveal where he hides his clothes, even though he knows that he would remain a wolf forever if he lost them or were caught putting them on (*kar si jes eusse perduz/e de ceo feusse aparceuz/bisclavret serei a tuz jours*). With the help of an accomplice who will become her lover, the woman takes the clothes from their hiding place, and the baron remains a wolf forever.

What is essential here is the detail, to which Pliny's legend of Antus also bears witness (*Natural History*, bk. 8), of the temporary character of the metamorphosis, which is tied to the possibility of setting aside and secretly putting on human clothes again. The transformation into a werewolf corresponds perfectly to the state of exception, during which (necessarily limited) time the city is dissolved and men enter into a zone in which they are no longer distinct from beasts. The story also shows the necessity of particular formalities marking the entry into—or the exit from—the zone of indistinction between the animal and the human (which corresponds to the clear proclamation of the state of exception as formally distinct from the rule). Contemporary folklore also bears witness to this necessity, in the three knocks on the door that the werewolf

who is becoming human again must make in order to be let into the
house:

> When they knock on the door the first time, the wife must not
> answer. If she did, she would see her husband still entirely as a wolf,
> and he would eat her and then run away into the forest forever. When
> they knock on the door the second time, the woman must still not
> answer: she would see him with a man's body and a wolf's head. Only
> when they knock on the door the third time can the door be opened:
> for only then are they completely transformed, only then has the wolf
> completely disappeared and has the man of before reappeared. (Levi,
> *Cristo si è fermato a Eboli,* pp. 104–5)

The special proximity of werewolf and sovereign too is ultimately
shown in the story. One day (so the lay tells), the king goes hunting in the
forest in which Bisclavret lives, and the dogs find the wolf-man as soon as
they are let loose. But as soon as Bisclavret sees the sovereign, he runs
toward him and grabs hold of his stirrup, licking his legs and his feet as if
he were imploring the king's mercy. Amazed at the beast's humanity
("this animal has wits and intelligence / . . . I will give my peace to the
beast / and for today I will hunt no more"), the king brings him to live
with him, and they become inseparable. The inevitable encounter with
the ex-wife and the punishment of the woman follow. What is important, however, is that Bisclavret's final transformation back into a human
takes place on the very bed of the sovereign.

The proximity of tyrant and wolf-man is also shown in Plato's *Republic,* in which the transformation of the guardian into a tyrant is
approximated to the Arcadian myth of Lycean Zeus:

> What, then, is the cause of the transformation of a protector into a
> tyrant? Is it not obviously when the protector's acts begin to reproduce
> the myth that is told of the shrine of Lycean Zeus in Arcadia? . . . The
> story goes that whoever tastes of one bit of human entrails minced up
> with those of other victims is inevitably transformed into a wolf. . . .
> Thus, when a leader of the mob [*dēmos*], seeing the multitude devoted
> to his orders, does not know how to abstain from the blood of his
> tribe . . . will it not then be necessary that he either be killed by his
> enemies or become a tyrant and be transformed from a man into a
> wolf? (*Republic,* 565d–565e)

6.3. The time has come, therefore, to reread from the beginning the myth of the foundation of the modern city from Hobbes to Rousseau. The state of nature is, in truth, a state of exception, in which the city appears for an instant (which is at the same time a chronological interval and a nontemporal moment) *tanquam dissoluta*. The foundation is thus not an event achieved once and for all but is continually operative in the civil state in the form of the sovereign decision. What is more, the latter refers *immediately* to the life (and not the free will) of the citizens, which thus appears as the originary political element, the *Urphänomen* of politics. Yet this life is not simply natural reproductive life, the *zoē* of the Greeks, nor *bios*, a qualified form of life. It is, rather, the bare life of *homo sacer* and the *wargus*, a zone of indistinction and continuous transition between man and beast, nature and culture.

This is why the thesis stated at the logico-formal level at the end of the first part above, according to which the originary juridico-political relation is the ban, not only is a thesis concerning the formal structure of sovereignty but also has a substantial character, since what the ban holds together is precisely bare life and sovereign power. All representations of the originary political act as a contract or convention marking the passage from nature to the State in a discrete and definite way must be left wholly behind. Here there is, instead, a much more complicated zone of indiscernability between *nomos* and *physis*, in which the State tie, having the form of a ban, is always already also non-State and pseudo-nature, and in which nature always already appears as *nomos* and the state of exception. The understanding of the Hobbesian mythologeme in terms of *contract* instead of *ban* condemned democracy to impotence every time it had to confront the problem of sovereign power and has also rendered modern democracy constitutionally incapable of truly thinking a politics freed from the form of the State.

The relation of abandonment is so ambiguous that nothing could be harder than breaking from it. The ban is essentially the power of delivering something over to itself, which is to say, the power of maintaining itself in relation to something presupposed as nonrelational. What has been banned is delivered over to its own separateness and, at the same time, consigned to the mercy of the one who abandons it—at once excluded and included, removed and at the same time captured. The age-old discussion in juridical historiography between those who conceive exile to be a punishment and those who instead understand it to be a right and a refuge (already at the end of the republic, Cicero thought exile in opposition to punishment: *Exilium enim non supplcium est, sed perfugium portusque supplicii*, "Exile is not a penalty, but a haven and a refuge from penalty" [*Pro Caec.*, 34]) has its root in this ambiguity of the sovereign ban. Both for Greece and for Rome, the oldest sources show that more ancient than the opposition between law and punishment is the status—which "cannot be qualified either as the exercise of a law or as a penal situation" (Crifò, *L'esclusione dall città*, p. 11)—of the person who goes into exile as a consequence of committing homicide, or who loses his citizenship as a result of becoming a citizen of a *civitas foederata* that benefits from an *ius exilii*.

The originary political relation is marked by this zone of indistinction in which the life of the exile or the *aqua et igni interdictus* borders on the life of *homo sacer*, who may be killed but not sacrificed. This relation is more original than the Schmittian opposition between friend and enemy, fellow citizen and foreigner. The "estrarity" of the person held in the sovereign ban is more intimate and primary than the extraneousness of the foreigner (if it is possible to develop in this way the opposition established by Festus between *extrarius*, which is to say, *qui extra focum sacramentum iusque sit* ["whoever is outside the hearth, the sacrament, and the law"], and *extraneus*, which is to say, *ex altera terra, quasi exterraneus* ["whoever is from another land and almost extraneous"]).

Now it is possible to understand the semantic ambiguity that we have already noted, in which "banned" in Romance languages originally meant both "at the mercy of" and "out of free will, freely," both "excluded, banned" and "open to all, free." The ban is the force of simultaneous attraction and repulsion that ties together the two poles of the sovereign exception: bare life and power, *homo sacer* and the sovereign. Because of this alone can the ban signify both the insignia of sovereignty (*Bandum, quod postea appellatus fuit Standardum, Guntfanonum, italice Confalone* [Muratori, *Antiquitates*, p. 442]) and expulsion from the community.

We must learn to recognize this structure of the ban in the political relations and public spaces in which we still live. *In the city, the banishment of sacred life is more internal than every interiority and more external than every extraneousness.* The banishment of sacred life is the sovereign *nomos* that conditions every rule, the originary spatialization that governs and makes possible every localization and every territorialization. And if in modernity life is more and more clearly placed at the center of State politics (which now becomes, in Foucault's terms, biopolitics), if in our age all citizens can be said, in a specific but extremely real sense, to appear virtually as *homines sacri*, this is possible only because the relation of ban has constituted the essential structure of sovereign power from the beginning.

§ Threshold

If the originally political element is sacred life, it becomes understandable how Bataille could have sought the fulfilled figure of sovereignty in life experienced in the extreme dimension of death, eroticism, excess, and the sacred, and yet also how Bataille could have failed to consider the link that binds that life to sovereign power. "The sovereignty of which I speak," he writes in the book bearing that name, which was conceived as the third section of *The Accursed Share*, "has little to do with that of states" (*La souveraineté*, p. 247). What Bataille is attempting to think here is clearly the very bare life (or sacred life) that, in the relation of ban, constitutes the immediate referent of sovereignty. And to have proposed the radical experience of this bare life is precisely what, despite everything, renders Bataille's effort exemplary. Unwittingly following the movement by which life as such comes to be what is at stake in modern political struggles, Bataille attempted to propose the very same bare life as a sovereign figure. And yet instead of recognizing bare life's eminently political (or rather biopolitical) nature, he inscribes the experience of this life both in the sphere of the sacred—which he understands, according to the dominant themes of the anthropology of his day taken up by Callois, as originarily ambivalent: pure and filthy, repugnant and fascinating—and in the interiority of the subject, to which the experience of this life is always given in privileged or miraculous moments. In the case of both ritual sacrifice and individual excess, sovereign life is defined for Bataille through the instantaneous transgression of the prohibition on killing.

In this way, Bataille immediately exchanges the political body of the sacred man, which can be killed but not sacrificed and which is inscribed in the logic of exception, for the prestige of the sacrificial body, which is defined instead by the logic of transgression. If Bataille's merit is to have brought to light the hidden link between bare life and sovereignty, albeit unknowingly, in his thought life still remains entirely bewitched in the ambiguous circle of the sacred. Bataille's work could offer only a real or farcical repetition of the sovereign ban, and it is understandable that Benjamin (according to Pierre Klossowski's account) stigmatized the Acéphale group's research with the peremptory phrase "You are working for fascism."

Not that Bataille does not discern that sacrifice is insufficient and that it is, in the last analysis, a "comedy." ("In sacrifice, the one being sacrificed identifies with the animal struck with death. Thus he dies watching himself die, and even by his own will, at peace with the weapon of sacrifice. But this is a comedy!" ["Hegel," p. 336].) Yet what Bataille is unable to master is precisely (as is shown by his interest in the pictures of the young Chinese torture victim, which he discusses in *The Tears of Eros*) the bare life of *homo sacer*, which the conceptual apparatus of sacrifice and eroticism cannot grasp.

It is Jean-Luc Nancy's achievement to have shown the ambiguity of Bataille's theory of sacrifice, and to have strongly affirmed the concept of an "unsacrificeable existence" against every sacrificial temptation. Yet if our analysis of *homo sacer* is correct, and the Bataillian definition of sovereignty with reference to transgression is inadequate with respect to the life in the sovereign ban that may be killed, then the concept of the "unsacrificeable" too must be seen as insufficient to grasp the violence at issue in modern biopolitics. *Homo sacer* is unsacrificeable, yet he may nevertheless be killed by anyone. The dimension of bare life that constitutes the immediate referent of sovereign violence is more original than the opposi-

tion of the sacrificeable and the unsacrificeable, and gestures toward an idea of sacredness that is no longer absolutely definable
through the conceptual pair (which is perfectly clear in societies
familiar with sacrifice) of fitness for sacrifice and immolation according to ritual forms. In modernity, the principle of the sacredness of life is thus completely emancipated from sacrificial ideology,
and in our culture the meaning of the term "sacred" continues the
semantic history of *homo sacer* and not that of sacrifice (and this is
why the demystifications of sacrificial ideology so common today
remain insufficient, even though they are correct). What confronts
us today is a life that as such is exposed to a violence without
precedent precisely in the most profane and banal ways. Our age is
the one in which a holiday weekend produces more victims on
Europe's highways than a war campaign, but to speak of a "sacredness of the highway railing" is obviously only an antiphrastic
definition (La Cecla, *Mente locale*, p. 115).

The wish to lend a sacrificial aura to the extermination of the
Jews by means of the term "Holocaust" was, from this perspective,
an irresponsible historiographical blindness. The Jew living under
Nazism is the privileged negative referent of the new biopolitical
sovereignty and is, as such, a flagrant case of a *homo sacer* in the
sense of a life that may be killed but not sacrificed. His killing
therefore constitutes, as we will see, neither capital punishment nor
a sacrifice, but simply the actualization of a mere "capacity to be
killed" inherent in the condition of the Jew as such. The truth—
which is difficult for the victims to face, but which we must have
the courage not to cover with sacrificial veils—is that the Jews were
exterminated not in a mad and giant holocaust but exactly as Hitler
had announced, "as lice," which is to say, as bare life. The dimension in which the extermination took place is neither religion nor
law, but biopolitics.

If it is true that the figure proposed by our age is that of an
unsacrificeable life that has nevertheless become capable of being
killed to an unprecedented degree, then the bare life of *homo sacer*
concerns us in a special way. Sacredness is a line of flight still

present in contemporary politics, a line that is as such moving into zones increasingly vast and dark, to the point of ultimately coinciding with the biological life itself of citizens. If today there is no longer any one clear figure of the sacred man, it is perhaps because we are all virtually *homines sacri*.

PART THREE

The Camp as Biopolitical Paradigm
of the Modern

§ 1 The Politicization of Life

1.1. In the last years of his life, while he was working on the history of sexuality and unmasking the deployments of power at work within it, Michel Foucault began to direct his inquiries with increasing insistence toward the study of what he defined as *biopolitics*, that is, the growing inclusion of man's natural life in the mechanisms and calculations of power. At the end of the first volume of *The History of Sexuality*, Foucault, as we have seen, summarizes the process by which life, at the beginning of the modern age, comes to be what is at stake in politics: "For millennia, man remained what he was for Aristotle: a living animal with the additional capacity for political existence; modern man is an animal whose politics calls his existence as a living being into question." Until the very end, however, Foucault continued to investigate the "processes of subjectivization" that, in the passage from the ancient to the modern world, bring the individual to objectify his own self, constituting himself as a subject and, at the same time, binding himself to a power of external control. Despite what one might have legitimately expected, Foucault never brought his insights to bear on what could well have appeared to be the exemplary place of modern biopolitics: the politics of the great totalitarian states of the twentieth century. The inquiry that began with a reconstruction of the *grand enfermement* in hospitals and prisons did not end with an analysis of the concentration camp.

If, on the other hand, the pertinent studies that Hannah Arendt dedicated to the structure of totalitarian states in the postwar period have a limit, it is precisely the absence of any biopolitical perspective. Arendt very clearly discerns the link between total-itarian rule and the particular condition of life that is the camp: "The supreme goal of all totalitarian states," she writes, in a plan for research on the concentration camps, which, unfortunately, was not carried through, "is not only the freely admitted, long-ranging ambition to global rule, but also the never admitted and imme-diately realized attempt at total domination. The concentration camps are the laboratories in the experiment of total domination, for human nature being what it is, this goal can be achieved only under the extreme circumstances of human made hell" (*Essays*, p. 240). Yet what escapes Arendt is that the process is in a certain sense the inverse of what she takes it to be, and that precisely the radical transformation of politics into the realm of bare life (that is, into a camp) legitimated and necessitated total domination. Only be-cause politics in our age had been entirely transformed into bio-politics was it possible for politics to be constituted as totalitarian politics to a degree hitherto unknown.

The fact that the two thinkers who may well have reflected most deeply on the political problem of our age were unable to link together their own insights is certainly an index of the difficulty of this problem. The concept of "bare life" or "sacred life" is the focal lens through which we shall try to make their points of view converge. In the notion of bare life the interlacing of politics and life has become so tight that it cannot easily be analyzed. Until we become aware of the political nature of bare life and its modern avatars (biological life, sexuality, etc.), we will not succeed in clarifying the opacity at their center. Conversely, once modern politics enters into an intimate symbiosis with bare life, it loses the intelligibility that still seems to us to characterize the juridico-political foundation of classical politics.

1.2. Karl Löwith was the first to define the fundamental charac-ter of totalitarian states as a "politicization of life" and, at the same time, to note the curious contiguity between democracy and totalitarianism:

> Since the emancipation of the third estate, the formation of bourgeois democracy and its transformation into mass industrial democracy, the neutralization of politically relevant differences and postponement of a decision about them has developed to the point of turning into its opposite: a total politicization [*totale Politisierung*] of everything, even of seemingly neutral domains of life. Thus in Marxist Russia there emerged a worker-state that was "more intensively state-oriented than any absolute monarchy"; in fascist Italy, a corporate state normatively regulating not only national work, but also "after-work" [*Dopolavoro*] and all spiritual life; and, in National Socialist Germany, a wholly integrated state, which, by means of racial laws and so forth, politicizes even the life that had until then been private. (*Der okkasionelle Dezionismus*, p. 33)

The contiguity between mass democracy and totalitarian states, nevertheless, does not have the form of a sudden transformation (as Löwith, here following in Schmitt's footsteps, seems to maintain); before impetuously coming to light in our century, the river of biopolitics that gave *homo sacer* his life runs its course in a hidden but continuous fashion. It is almost as if, starting from a certain point, every decisive political event were double-sided: the spaces, the liberties, and the rights won by individuals in their conflicts with central powers always simultaneously prepared a tacit but increasing inscription of individuals' lives within the state order, thus offering a new and more dreadful foundation for the very sovereign power from which they wanted to liberate themselves. "The 'right' to life," writes Foucault, explaining the importance assumed by sex as a political issue, "to one's body, to health, to happiness, to the satisfaction of needs and, beyond all the oppressions or 'alienation,' the 'right' to rediscover what one is and all that one can be, this 'right'—which the classical juridical system was utterly incapable of comprehending—was the political response to all these new procedures of power" (*La volonté*, p. 191). The fact is that one and the same affirmation of bare life leads, in bourgeois democracy, to a primacy of the private over the public and of individual liberties over collective obligations and yet becomes, in totalitarian states, the decisive political criterion and the exemplary realm of sovereign decisions. And only because biological life and its needs had become the *politically* decisive fact is it possible to understand the otherwise incomprehensible rapidity with which twentieth-century parliamentary democracies were able to turn into totalitarian states and with which this century's totalitarian states were able to be converted, almost without interruption, into parliamentary democracies. In both cases, these transformations were produced in a context in which for quite some time politics had already turned into biopolitics, and in which the only real question to be decided was which form of organization would be best suited to the task of assuring the care, control, and use of bare life. Once their fundamental referent becomes bare life, traditional political distinctions (such as those between Right and Left, liberalism and totalitarianism, private and public) lose their clarity and intelligibility and enter into a zone of indistinction. The ex-communist ruling classes' unexpected fall into the most extreme racism (as in the Serbian program of "ethnic cleansing") and the rebirth of new forms of fascism in Europe also have their roots here.

Along with the emergence of biopolitics, we can observe a displacement and gradual expansion beyond the limits of the decision on bare life, in the state of exception, in which sovereignty consisted. If there is a line in every modern state marking the point at which the decision on life becomes a decision on death, and biopolitics can turn into thanatopolitics, this line no longer appears today as a stable border dividing two clearly distinct zones. This line is now in motion and gradually moving into areas other than that of political life, areas in which the sovereign is entering into an ever more intimate symbiosis not only with the jurist but also with the doctor, the scientist, the expert, and the priest. In the pages that follow, we shall try to show that certain events that are fundamental for the political history of modernity (such as the declaration of rights), as well as others that seem instead to represent an incomprehensible intrusion of biologico-scientific principles into the political order (such as National Socialist eugenics and its elimination of "life that is unworthy of being lived," or the contemporary debate on the normative determination of death criteria), acquire their true sense only if they are brought back to the common biopolitical (or thanatopolitical) context to which they belong. From this perspective, the camp—as the pure, absolute, and impassable biopolitical space (insofar as it is founded solely on the state of exception)—will appear as the hidden paradigm of the political space of modernity, whose metamorphoses and disguises we will have to learn to recognize.

1.3. The first recording of bare life as the new political subject is already implicit in the document that is generally placed at the foundation of modern democracy: the 1679 writ of *habeas corpus*. Whatever the origin of this formula, used as early as the eighteenth century to assure the physical presence of a person before a court of justice, it is significant that at its center is neither the old subject of feudal relations and liberties nor the future *citoyen*, but rather a pure and simple *corpus*. When John the Landless conceded Magna Carta to his subjects in 1215, he turned his attention to the "archbishops, bishops, abbots, counts, barons, viscounts, provosts, officials and bailiffs," to the "cities, towns, villages," and, more generally, to the "free men of our kingdom," so that they might enjoy "their ancient liberties and free customs" as well as the ones he now specifically recognized. Article 29, whose task was to guarantee the physical freedom of the subjects, reads: "No free man [*homo liber*] may be arrested, imprisoned, dispossessed of his goods, or placed outside the law [*utlagetur*] or molested in any way; we will not place our hands on him nor will have others place their hands on him [*nec super eum ibimis, nec super eum mittimusi*], except after a legal judgment by his peers according to the law of the realm." Analogously, an ancient writ that preceded the *habeas corpus* and was understood to assure the presence of the accused in a trial bears the title *de homine replegiando* (or *repigliando*).

Consider instead the formula of the writ that the act of 1679 generalizes and makes into law: *Praecipimus tibi quod Corpus X, in custodia vestra detentum, ut dicitur, una cum causa captionis et detentionis, quodcumque nomine idem X censeatur in eadem, habeas coram nobis, apud Westminster, ad subjiciendum,* "We command that you have before us to show, at Westminster, that body X, by whatsoever name he may be called therein, which is held in your custody, as it is said, as well as the cause of the arrest and the detention." Nothing allows one to measure the difference between ancient and medieval freedom and the freedom at the basis of modern democracy better than this formula. It is not the free man and his statutes and prerogatives, nor even simply *homo,* but rather *corpus* that is the new subject of politics. And democracy is born precisely as the assertion and presentation of this "body": *habeas corpus ad subjiciendum,* "you will have to have a body to show."

The fact that, of the all the various jurisdictional regulations concerned with the protection of individual freedom, it was *habeas corpus* that assumed the form of law and thus became inseparable from the history of Western democracy is surely due to mere circumstance. It is just as certain, however, that nascent European democracy thereby placed at the center of its battle against absolutism not *bios,* the qualified life of the citizen, but *zoē*—the bare, anonymous life that is as such taken into the sovereign ban ("the body of being taken . . . ," as one still reads in one modern formulation of the writ, "by whatsoever name he may be called therein").

What comes to light in order to be exposed *apud Westminster* is, once again, the body of *homo sacer,* which is to say, bare life. This is modern democracy's strength and, at the same time, its inner contradiction: modern democracy does not abolish sacred life but rather shatters it and disseminates it into every individual body, making it into what is at stake in political conflict. And the root of modern democracy's secret biopolitical calling lies here: he who will appear later as the bearer of rights and, according to a curious oxymoron, as the new sovereign subject (*subiectus superaneus,* in other words, what is below and, at the same time, most elevated) can only be constituted as such through the repetition of the sovereign exception and the isolation of *corpus,* bare life, in himself. If it is true that law needs a body in order to be in force, and if one can speak, in this sense, of "law's desire to have a body," democracy responds to this desire by compelling law to assume the care of this body. This ambiguous (or polar) character of democracy appears even more clearly in the *habeas corpus* if one considers the fact that the same legal procedure that was originally intended to assure the presence of the accused at the trial and, therefore, to keep the accused from avoiding judgment, turns—in its new and definitive form—into grounds for the sheriff to detain and exhibit the body of the accused. *Corpus is a two-faced being, the bearer both of subjection to sovereign power and of individual liberties.*

This new centrality of the "body" in the sphere of politico-juridical terminology thus coincides with the more general process by which *corpus* is given such a privileged position in the philosophy and science of the Baroque age, from Descartes to Newton, from Leibniz to Spinoza. And yet in political reflection *corpus* always maintains a close tie to bare life, even when it becomes the central metaphor of the political community, as in *Leviathan* or *The Social Contract.* Hobbes's use of the term is particularly instructive in this regard. If it is true that in *De homine* he distinguishes man's natural body from his political body (*homo enim non modo corpus naturale est, sed etiam civitatis, id est, ut ita loquar, corporis politici pars,* "Man is not only a natural body, but also a body of the city, that is, of the so-called political part" [*De homine*, p. 1]), in the *De cive* it is precisely the body's capacity to be killed that founds both the natural equality of men and the necessity of the "Commonwealth":

> If we look at adult men and consider the fragility of the unity of the human body (whose ruin marks the end of every strength, vigor, and force) and the ease with which the weakest man can kill the strongest man, there is no reason for someone to trust in his strength and think himself superior to others by nature. Those who can do the same things to each other are equals. And those who can do the supreme thing— that is, kill—are by nature equal among themselves. (*De cive*, p. 93)

The great metaphor of the Leviathan, whose body is formed out of all the bodies of individuals, must be read in this light. The absolute capacity of the subjects' bodies to be killed forms the new political body of the West.

§ 2   Biopolitics and the Rights of Man

2.1. Hannah Arendt entitled the fifth chapter of her book on imperialism, which is dedicated to the problem of refugees, "The Decline of the Nation-State and the End of the Rights of Man." Linking together the fates of the rights of man and of the nation-state, her striking formulation seems to imply the idea of an intimate and necessary connection between the two, though the author herself leaves the question open. The paradox from which Arendt departs is that the very figure who should have embodied the rights of man par excellence—the refugee—signals instead the concept's radical crisis. "The conception of human rights," she states, "based upon the assumed existence of a human being as such, broke down at the very moment when those who professed to believe in it were for the first time confronted with people who had indeed lost all other qualities and specific relationships—except that they were still human" (*Origins*, p. 299). In the system of the nation-state, the so-called sacred and inalienable rights of man show themselves to lack every protection and reality at the moment in which they can no longer take the form of rights belonging to citizens of a state. If one considers the matter, this is in fact implicit in the ambiguity of the very title of the French Declaration of the Rights of Man and Citizen, of 1789. In the phrase *La déclaration des droits de l'homme et du citoyen*, it is not clear whether the two terms *homme* and *citoyen* name two autonomous beings or instead form a unitary system in which the first is always already included in the second. And if the latter is the case, the kind of relation that exists between *homme* and *citoyen* still remains unclear. From this perspective, Burke's *boutade* according to which he preferred his "Rights of an Englishman" to the inalienable rights of man acquires an unsuspected profundity.

Arendt does no more than offer a few, essential hints concerning the link between the rights of man and the nation-state, and her suggestion has therefore not been followed up. In the period after the Second World War, both the instrumental emphasis on the rights of man and the rapid growth of declarations and agreements on the part of international organizations have ultimately made any authentic understanding of the historical significance of the phenomenon almost impossible. Yet it is time to stop regarding declarations of rights as proclamations of eternal, metajuridical values binding the legislator (in fact, without much success) to respect eternal ethical principles, and to begin to consider them according to their real historical function in the modern nation-state. Declarations of rights represent the originary figure of the inscription of natural life in the juridico-political order of the nation-state. The same bare life that in the *ancien régime* was politically neutral and belonged to God as creaturely life and in the classical world was (at least apparently) clearly distinguished as *zoē* from political life (*bios*) now fully enters into the structure of the state and even becomes the earthly foundation of the state's legitimacy and sovereignty.

A simple examination of the text of the Declaration of 1789 shows that it is precisely bare natural life—which is to say, the pure fact of birth—that appears here as the source and bearer of rights. "Men," the first article declares, "are born and remain free and equal in rights" (from this perspective, the strictest formulation of all is to be found in La Fayette's project elaborated in July 1789: "Every man is born with inalienable and indefeasible rights"). At the same time, however, the very natural life that, inaugurating the biopolitics of modernity, is placed at the foundation of the order vanishes into the figure of the citizen, in whom rights are "preserved" (according to the second article: "The goal of every political association is the preservation of the natural and indefeasible rights of man"). And the Declaration can attribute sovereignty to the "nation" (according to the third article: "The principle of all sovereignty resides essentially in the nation") precisely because it has already inscribed this element of birth in the very heart of the political community. The nation—the term derives etymologically from *nascere* (to be born)—thus closes the open circle of man's birth.

2.2. Declarations of rights must therefore be viewed as the place in which the passage from divinely authorized royal sovereignty to national sovereignty is accomplished. This passage assures the *exceptio* of life in the new state order that will succeed the collapse of the *ancien régime*. The fact that in this process the "subject" is, as has been noted, transformed into a "citizen" means that birth— which is to say, bare natural life as such—here for the first time becomes (thanks to a transformation whose biopolitical consequences we are only beginning to discern today) the immediate bearer of sovereignty. The principle of nativity and the principle of sovereignty, which were separated in the *ancien régime* (where birth marked only the emergence of a *sujet*, a subject), are now irrevocably united in the body of the "sovereign subject" so that the foundation of the new nation-state may be constituted. It is not possible to understand the "national" and biopolitical development and vocation of the modern state in the nineteenth and twentieth centuries if one forgets that what lies at its basis is not man as a free and conscious political subject but, above all, man's bare life, the simple birth that as such is, in the passage from subject to citizen, invested with the principle of sovereignty. The fiction implicit here is that *birth* immediately becomes *nation* such that there can be no interval of separation [*scarto*] between the two terms. Rights are attributed to man (or originate in him) solely to the extent that man is the immediately vanishing ground (who must never come to light as such) of the citizen.

Only if we understand this essential historical function of the doctrine of rights can we grasp the development and metamorphosis of declarations of rights in our century. When the hidden difference [*scarto*] between birth and nation entered into a lasting crisis following the devastation of Europe's geopolitical order after the First World War, what appeared was Nazism and fascism, that is, two properly biopolitical movements that made of natural life the exemplary place of the sovereign decision. We are used to condensing the essence of National Socialist ideology into the syntagm "blood and soil" (*Blut und Boden*). When Alfred Rosenberg wanted to express his party's vision of the world, it is precisely to this hendiadys that he turned. "The National Socialist vision of the world," he writes, "springs from the conviction that soil and blood constitute what is essential about Germanness, and that it is therefore in reference to these two givens that a cultural and state politics must be directed" (*Blut und Ehre*, p. 242). Yet it has too often been forgotten that this formula, which is so highly determined politically, has, in truth, an innocuous juridical origin. The formula is nothing other than the concise expression of the two criteria that, already in Roman law, served to identify citizenship (that is, the primary inscription of life in the state order): *ius soli* (birth in a certain territory) and *ius sanguinis* (birth from citizen parents). In the *ancien régime*, these two traditional juridical criteria had no essential meaning, since they expressed only a relation of subjugation. Yet with the French Revolution they acquire a new and decisive importance. Citizenship now does not simply identify a generic subjugation to royal authority or a determinate system of laws, nor does it simply embody (as Chalier maintained when he suggested to the convention on September 23, 1792, that the title of citizen be substituted for the traditional title *monsieur* or *sieur* in every public act) the new egalitarian principle; citizenship names the new status of life as origin and ground of sovereignty and, therefore, literally identifies—to cite Jean-Denis Lanjuinais's words to the convention—*les membres du souverain*, "the members of the sovereign." Hence the centrality (and the ambiguity) of the notion of "citizenship" in modern political thought, which compels Rousseau to say, "No author in France . . . has understood the true meaning of the term 'citizen.'" Hence too, however, the rapid

growth in the course of the French Revolution of regulatory provi-
sions specifying which *man* was a *citizen* and which one not, and
articulating and gradually restricting the area of the *ius soli* and the
ius sanguinis. Until this time, the questions "What is French? What
is German?" had constituted not a political problem but only one
theme among others discussed in philosophical anthropologies.
Caught in a constant work of redefinition, these questions now
begin to become essentially political, to the point that, with National Socialism, the answer to the question "Who and what is
German?" (and also, therefore, "Who and what is not German?")
coincides immediately with the highest political task. Fascism and
Nazism are, above all, redefinitions of the relations between man
and citizen, and become fully intelligible only when situated—no
matter how paradoxical it may seem—in the biopolitical context
inaugurated by national sovereignty and declarations of rights.

Only this tie between the rights of man and the new biopolitical
determination of sovereignty makes it possible to understand the
striking fact, which has often been noted by historians of the
French Revolution, that at the very moment in which native rights
were declared to be inalienable and indefeasible, the rights of man
in general were divided into active rights and passive rights. In his
Préliminaires de la constitution, Sieyès already clearly stated:

> Natural and civil rights are those rights *for* whose preservation society
> is formed, and political rights are those rights *by* which society is
> formed. For the sake of clarity, it would be best to call the first ones
> passive rights, and the second ones active rights. . . . All inhabitants of
> a country must enjoy the rights of passive citizens . . . all are not active
> citizens. Women, at least in the present state, children, foreigners, and
> also those who would not at all contribute to the public establishment
> must have no active influence on public matters. (*Écrits politiques*, pp.
> 189–206)

And after defining the *membres du souverain*, the passage of Lanjuinais cited above continues with these words: "Thus children, the
insane, minors, women, those condemned to a punishment either
restricting personal freedom or bringing disgrace [*punition afflic-*

tive ou inflammante] . . . will not be citizens" (quoted in Sewell, "Le citoyen," p. 105).

Instead of viewing these distinctions as a simple restriction of the democratic and egalitarian principle, in flagrant contradiction to the spirit and letter of the declarations, we ought first to grasp their coherent biopolitical meaning. One of the essential characteristics of modern biopolitics (which will continue to increase in our century) is its constant need to redefine the threshold in life that distinguishes and separates what is inside from what is outside. Once it crosses over the walls of the *oikos* and penetrates more and more deeply into the city, the foundation of sovereignty—nonpolitical life—is immediately transformed into a line that must be constantly redrawn. Once *zoē* is politicized by declarations of rights, the distinctions and thresholds that make it possible to isolate a sacred life must be newly defined. And when natural life is wholly included in the *polis*—and this much has, by now, already happened—these thresholds pass, as we will see, beyond the dark boundaries separating life from death in order to identify a new living dead man, a new sacred man.

2.3. If refugees (whose number has continued to grow in our century, to the point of including a significant part of humanity today) represent such a disquieting element in the order of the modern nation-state, this is above all because by breaking the continuity between man and citizen, *nativity* and *nationality*, they put the originary fiction of modern sovereignty in crisis. Bringing to light the difference between birth and nation, the refugee causes the secret presupposition of the political domain—bare life—to appear for an instant within that domain. In this sense, the refugee is truly "the man of rights," as Arendt suggests, the first and only real appearance of rights outside the fiction of the citizen that always covers them over. Yet this is precisely what makes the figure of the refugee so hard to define politically.

Since the First World War, the birth-nation link has no longer been capable of performing its legitimating function inside the nation-state, and the two terms have begun to show themselves to be irreparably loosened from each other. From this perspective, the immense increase of refugees and stateless persons in Europe (in a short span of time 1,500,000 White Russians, 700,000 Armenians, 500,000 Bulgarians, 1,000,000 Greeks, and hundreds of thousands of Germans, Hungarians, and Rumanians were displaced from their countries) is one of the two most significant phenomena. The other is the contemporaneous institution by many European states of juridical measures allowing for the mass denaturalization and denationalization of large portions of their own populations. The first introduction of such rules into the juridical order took place in France in 1915 with respect to naturalized citizens of "enemy" origin; in 1922, Belgium followed the French example and revoked the naturalization of citizens who had committed "antinational" acts during the war; in 1926, the fascist regime issued an analogous law with respect to citizens who had shown themselves to be "unworthy of Italian citizenship"; in 1933, it was Austria's turn; and so it continued until the Nuremberg laws on "citizenship in the Reich" and the "protection of German blood and honor" brought this process to the most extreme point of its development, introducing the principle according to which citizenship was something of which one had to prove oneself worthy and which could therefore always be called into question. And one of the few rules to which the Nazis constantly adhered during the course of the "Final Solution" was that Jews could be sent to the extermination camps only after they had been fully denationalized (stripped even of the residual citizenship left to them after the Nuremberg laws).

These two phenomena—which are, after all, absolutely correlative—show that the birth-nation link, on which the declaration of 1789 had founded national sovereignty, had already lost its mechanical force and power of self-regulation by the time of the First World War. On the one hand, the nation-states become greatly concerned with natural life, discriminating within it between a so-to-speak authentic life and a life lacking every political value. (Nazi racism and eugenics are only comprehensible if they are brought back to this context.) On the other hand, the very rights of man that once made sense as the presupposition of the rights of the citizen are now progressively separated from and used outside the context of citizenship, for the sake of the supposed representation and protection of a bare life that is more and more driven to the margins of the nation-states, ultimately to be recodified into a new national identity. The contradictory character of these processes is certainly one of the reasons for the failure of the attempts of the various committees and organizations by which states, the League of Nations, and, later, the United Nations confronted the problem of refugees and the protection of human rights, from the Bureau Nansen (1922) to the contemporary High Commission for Refugees (1951), whose actions, according to statute, are to have not a political but rather a "solely humanitarian and social" mission. What is essential is that, every time refugees represent not individual cases but—as happens more and more often today—a mass phenomenon, both these organizations and individual states prove themselves, despite their solemn invocations of the "sacred and inalienable" rights of man, absolutely incapable of resolving the problem and even of confronting it adequately.

2.4. The separation between humanitarianism and politics that we are experiencing today is the extreme phase of the separation of the rights of man from the rights of the citizen. In the final analysis, however, humanitarian organizations—which today are more and more supported by international commissions—can only grasp human life in the figure of bare or sacred life, and therefore, despite themselves, maintain a secret solidarity with the very powers they ought to fight. It takes only a glance at the recent publicity campaigns to gather funds for refugees from Rwanda to realize that here human life is exclusively considered (and there are certainly good reasons for this) as sacred life—which is to say, as life that can be killed but not sacrificed—and that only as such is it made into the object of aid and protection. The "imploring eyes" of the Rwandan child, whose photograph is shown to obtain money but who "is now becoming more and more difficult to find alive," may well be the most telling contemporary cipher of the bare life that humanitarian organizations, in perfect symmetry with state power, need. A humanitarianism separated from politics cannot fail to reproduce the isolation of sacred life at the basis of sovereignty, and the camp—which is to say, the pure space of exception—is the biopolitical paradigm that it cannot master.

The concept of the refugee (and the figure of life that this concept represents) must be resolutely separated from the concept of the rights of man, and we must seriously consider Arendt's claim that the fates of human rights and the nation-state are bound together such that the decline and crisis of the one necessarily implies the end of the other. The refugee must be considered for what he is: nothing less than a limit concept that radically calls into question the fundamental categories of the nation-state, from the birth-nation to the man-citizen link, and that thereby makes it possible to clear the way for a long-overdue renewal of categories in the service of a politics in which bare life is no longer separated and excepted, either in the state order or in the figure of human rights.

א The pamphlet *Make More of an Effort, Frenchmen, if You Want to Be Republicans*, read by the libertine Dolmancé in the Marquis de Sade's *Philosophy in the Boudoir*, is the first and perhaps most radical biopolitical manifesto of modernity. At the very moment in which the revolution makes birth—which is to say, bare life—into the foundation of sovereignty and rights, Sade stages (in his entire work, and in particular in *120 Days of Sodom*) the *theatrum politicum* as a theater of bare life, in which the very physiological life of bodies appears, through sexuality, as the pure political element. But the political meaning of Sade's work is nowhere as explicit as it is in this pamphlet, in which the *maisons* in which every citizen can publicly summon any other citizen in order to compel him to satisfy his own needs emerge as the political realm par excellence. Not only philosophy (Lefort, *Écrire*, pp. 100–101) but also and above all politics is sifted through the boudoir. Indeed, in Dolmancé's project, the boudoir fully takes the place of the *cité*, in a dimension in which the public and the private, political existence and bare life change places.

The growing importance of sadomasochism in modernity has its root in this exchange. Sadomasochism is precisely the technique of sexuality by which the bare life of a sexual partner is brought to light. Not only does Sade consciously invoke the analogy with sovereign power ("there is no man," he writes, "who does not want to be a despot when he has an erection"), but we also find here the symmetry between *homo sacer* and sovereign, in the complicity that ties the masochist to the sadist, the victim to the executioner.

Sade's modernity does not consist in his having foreseen the unpolitical primacy of sexuality in our unpolitical age. On the contrary, Sade is as contemporary as he is because of his incomparable presentation of the absolutely political (that is, "biopolitical") meaning of sexuality and physiological life itself. Like the concentration camps of our century, the totalitarian character of the organization of life in Silling's castle—with its meticulous regulations that do not spare any aspect of physiological life (not even the digestive function, which is obsessively codified and publicized)—has its root in the fact that what is proposed here for the first time is a normal and collective (and hence political) organization of human life founded solely on bare life.

§ 3 Life That Does Not Deserve to Live

3.1. In 1920, Felix Meiner, one of the most distinguished German publishers of philosophical works, released a blue-gray *plaquette* bearing the title *Authorization for the Annihilation of Life Unworthy of Being Lived* (*Die Freigabe der Vernichtung lebensunwerten Lebens*). The authors were Karl Binding, a highly respected specialist of penal law (an insert attached to the jacket cover at the last minute informed readers that since the *doct. iur. et phil.* K. B. had passed away during the printing of the work, the publication was to be considered as "his last act for the good of humanity"), and Alfred Hoche, a professor of medicine whose interest lay in questions concerning the ethics of his profession.

The book warrants our attention for two reasons. The first is that in order to explain the unpunishability of suicide, Binding is led to conceive of suicide as the expression of man's sovereignty over his own existence. Since suicide, he argues, cannot be understood as a crime (for example, as a violation of a duty toward oneself) yet also cannot be considered as a matter of indifference to the law, "the law has no other option than to consider living man as sovereign over his own existence [*als Souverän über sein Dasein*]" (*Die Freigabe*, p. 14). Like the sovereign decision on the state of exception, the sovereignty of the living being over himself takes the form of a threshold of indiscernibility between exteriority and interiority, which the juridical order can therefore neither exclude nor include, neither forbid nor permit: "The juridical order," Binding writes, "tolerates the act despite the actual consequences that it must itself suffer on account of it. It does not claim to have the power to forbid it" (ibid.).

Yet from this particular sovereignty of man over his own existence, Binding derives—and this is the second, and more urgent, reason for our interest in this book—the necessity of authorizing "the annihilation of life unworthy of being lived." The fact that Binding uses this disquieting expression to designate merely the problem of the lawfulness of euthanasia should not lead one to underestimate the novelty and decisive importance of the concept that here makes its first appearance on the European juridical scene: life that does not deserve to be lived (or to live, as the German expression *lebensunwerten Leben* also quite literally suggests), along with its implicit and more familiar correlate—life that deserves to be lived (or to live). The fundamental biopolitical structure of modernity—the decision on the value (or nonvalue) of life as such—therefore finds its first juridical articulation in a well-intentioned pamphlet in favor of euthanasia.

א It is not surprising that Binding's essay aroused the curiosity of Schmitt, who cites it in his *Theorie des Partisanen* in the context of a critique of the introduction of the concept of value into law. "He who determines a value," Schmitt writes, "*eo ipso* always fixes a nonvalue. The sense of this determination of a nonvalue is the annihilation of the nonvalue" (p. 80, n. 49). Schmitt approximates Binding's theories concerning life that does not deserve to live to Heinrich Rickert's idea that "negation is the criterion by which to establish whether something belongs to the sphere of value" and that "the true act of evaluation is negation." Here Schmitt does not seem to notice that the logic of value he is criticizing resembles his own theory of sovereignty, according to which the true life of the rule is the exception.

3.2. For Binding the concept of "life unworthy of being lived" is essential, since it allows him to find an answer to the juridical question he wishes to pose: "Must the unpunishability of the killing of life remain limited to suicide, as it is in contemporary law (with the exception of the state of emergency), or must it be extended to the killing of third parties?" According to Binding, the solution depends on the answer to the following question: "Are there human lives that have so lost the quality of legal good that their very existence no longer has any value, either for the person leading such a life or for society?" Binding continues:

> Whoever poses this question seriously must, with bitterness, notice the irresponsibility with which we usually treat the lives that are most full of value [*wertvollsten Leben*], as well as with what—often completely useless—care, patience, and energy we attempt, on the other hand, to keep in existence lives that are no longer worthy of being lived, to the point at which nature herself, often with cruel belatedness, takes away any possibility of their continuation. Imagine a battle camp covered with thousands of young bodies without life, or a mine where a catastrophe has killed hundreds of industrious workers, and at the same time picture our institutes for the mentally impaired [*Idioteninstitut*] and the treatments they lavish on their patients—for then one cannot help being shaken up by this sinister contrast between the sacrifice of the dearest human good and, on the other hand, the enormous care for existences that not only are devoid of value [*wertlosen*] but even ought to be valued negatively. (*Die Freigabe*, pp. 27–29)

The concept of "life devoid of value" (or "life unworthy of being lived") applies first of all to individuals who must be considered as "incurably lost" following an illness or an accident and who, fully conscious of their condition, desire "redemption" (Binding uses the term *Erlösung*, which belongs to religious language and signifies, among other things, redemption) and have somehow communicated this desire. More problematic is the condition of the second group, comprising "incurable idiots, either those born as such or those—for example, those who suffer from progressive paralysis—who have become such in the last phase of their life." "These men," Binding writes, "have neither the will to live nor the will to die. On the one hand, there is no ascertainable consent to die; on the other hand, their killing does not infringe upon any will to live that must be overcome. Their life is absolutely without purpose, but they do not find it to be intolerable." Even in this case, Binding sees no reason, "be it juridical, social, or religious, not to authorize the killing of these men, who are nothing but the frightening reverse image [*Gegenbild*] of authentic humanity" (ibid., pp. 31–32). As to the problem of who is competent to authorize annihilation, Binding proposes that the request for the initiative be made by the ill person himself (when he is capable of it) or by a doctor or a close relative, and that the final decision fall to a state committee composed of a doctor, a psychiatrist, and a jurist.

3.3. It is not our intention here to take a position on the difficult ethical problem of euthanasia, which still today, in certain countries, occupies a substantial position in medical debates and provokes disagreement. Nor are we concerned with the radicality with which Binding declares himself in favor of the general admissibility of euthanasia. More interesting for our inquiry is the fact that the sovereignty of the living man over his own life has its immediate counterpart in the determination of a threshold beyond which life ceases to have any juridical value and can, therefore, be killed without the commission of a homicide. The new juridical category of "life devoid of value" (or "life unworthy of being lived") corresponds exactly—even if in an apparently different direction—to the bare life of *homo sacer* and can easily be extended beyond the limits imagined by Binding.

It is as if every valorization and every "politicization" of life (which, after all, is implicit in the sovereignty of the individual over his own existence) necessarily implies a new decision concerning the threshold beyond which life ceases to be politically relevant, becomes only "sacred life," and can as such be eliminated without punishment. Every society sets this limit; every society—even the most modern—decides who its "sacred men" will be. It is even possible that this limit, on which the politicization and the *exceptio* of natural life in the juridical order of the state depends, has done nothing but extend itself in the history of the West and has now—in the new biopolitical horizon of states with national sovereignty—

moved inside every human life and every citizen. Bare life is no
longer confined to a particular place or a definite category. It now
dwells in the biological body of every living being.

3.4. During the physicians' trial at Nuremberg, a witness, Dr.
Fritz Mennecke, related that he had heard Drs. Hevelemann,
Bahnen, and Brack communicate in a confidential meeting in
Berlin in February 1940 that the Reich had just issued measures
authorizing "the elimination of life unworthy of being lived" with
special reference to the incurable mentally ill. The information was
not quite exact, since for various reasons Hitler preferred not to
give an explicit legal form to his euthanasia program. Yet it is
certain that the reappearance of the formula coined by Binding to
give juridical credence to the so-called "mercy killing" or "death by
grace" (*Gnadentod,* according to a euphemism common among the
regime's health officials) coincides with a decisive development in
National Socialism's biopolitics.

There is no reason to doubt that the "humanitarian" considerations that led Hitler and Himmler to elaborate a euthanasia program immediately after their rise to power were in good faith, just
as Binding and Hoche, from their own point of view, acted in good
faith in proposing the concept of "life unworthy of being lived."
For a variety of reasons, including foreseen opposition from Christian organizations, the program barely went into effect, and only at
the start of 1940 did Hitler decide that it could no longer be de-
layed. The Euthanasia Program for the Incurably Ill (*Euthanasie-
Programm für unheilbaren Kranke*) was therefore put into practice
in conditions—including the war economy and the increasing
growth of concentration camps for Jews and other undesirables—
that favored misuse and mistakes. Nevertheless, the transformation
of the program, over the course of the fifteen months it lasted
(Hitler ended it in August 1941 because of growing protest on the
part of bishops and relatives), from a theoretically humanitarian
program into a work of mass extermination did not in any way
depend simply on circumstance. The name of Grafeneck, the town
in Württemberg that was the home of one of the main centers, has

remained sadly linked to this matter, but analogous institutions existed in Hadamer (Hesse), Hartheim (near Linz), and other towns in the Reich. Testimony given by defendants and witnesses at the Nuremberg trials give us sufficiently precise information concerning the organization of the Grafeneck program. Every day, the medical center received about 70 people (from the ages of 6 to 93 years old) who had been chosen from the incurably mentally ill throughout German mental hospitals. Drs. Schumann and Baumhardt, who were responsible for the Grafeneck center, gave the patients a summary examination and then decided if they met the requirements specified by the program. In most cases, the patients were killed within 24 hours of their arrival at Grafeneck. First they were given a 2-centimeter dose of Morphium-Scopolamine; then they were sent to a gas chamber. In other institutions (for example in Hadamer), the patients were killed with a strong dose of Luminal, Veronal, and Morphium. It is calculated that 60,000 people were killed this way.

3.5. Some have referred to the eugenic principles that guided National Socialist biopolitics to explain the tenacity with which Hitler promoted his euthanasia program in such unfavorable circumstances. From a strictly eugenic point of view, however, euthanasia was not all necessary; not only did the laws on the prevention of hereditary diseases and on the protection of the hereditary health of the German people already provide a sufficient defense against genetic mental illnesses, but the incurably ill subjected to the program—mainly children and the elderly—were, in any case, in no condition to reproduce themselves (from a eugenic point of view, what is important is obviously not the elimination of the phenotype but only the elimination of the genetic set). Moreover, there is absolutely no reason to think that the program was linked to economic considerations. On the contrary, the program constituted a significant organizational burden at a time when the state apparatus was completely occupied with the war effort. Why then did Hitler want the program to be put into effect at all costs, when he was fully conscious of its unpopularity?

The only explanation left is that the program, in the guise of a solution to a humanitarian problem, was an exercise of the sovereign power to decide on bare life in the horizon of the new biopolitical vocation of the National Socialist state. The concept of "life unworthy of being lived" is clearly not an ethical one, which would involve the expectations and legitimate desires of the individual. It is, rather, a political concept in which what is at issue is the extreme metamorphosis of sacred life—which may be killed but not sacrificed—on which sovereign power is founded. If euthanasia lends itself to this exchange, it is because in euthanasia one man finds himself in the position of having to separate *zoē* and *bios* in another man, and to isolate in him something like a bare life that may be killed. From the perspective of modern biopolitics, however, euthanasia is situated at the intersection of the sovereign decision on life that may be killed and the assumption of the care of the nation's biological body. Euthanasia signals the point at which biopolitics necessarily turns into thanatopolitics.

Here it becomes clear how Binding's attempt to transform euthanasia into a juridico-political concept ("life unworthy of being lived") touched on a crucial matter. If it is the sovereign who, insofar as he decides on the state of exception, has the power to decide which life may be killed without the commission of homicide, in the age of biopolitics this power becomes emancipated from the state of exception and transformed into the power to decide the point at which life ceases to be politically relevant. When life becomes the supreme political value, not only is the problem of life's nonvalue thereby posed, as Schmitt suggests but further, it is as if the ultimate ground of sovereign power were at stake in this decision. In modern biopolitics, sovereign is he who decides on the value or the nonvalue of life as such. Life—which, with the declarations of rights, had as such been invested with the principle of sovereignty—now itself becomes the place of a sovereign decision. The Führer represents precisely life itself insofar as it is he who decides on life's very biopolitical consistency. This is why the Führer's word, according to a theory dear to Nazi jurists to which we will return, is immediately law. This is why the problem of euthanasia is an absolutely modern problem, which Nazism, as the first radically biopolitical state, could not fail to pose. And this is also why certain apparent confusions and contradictions of the euthanasia program can be explained only in the biopolitical context in which they were situated.

The physicians Karl Brand and Viktor Brack, who were sentenced to death at Nuremberg for being responsible for the program, declared after their condemnation that they did not feel guilty, since the problem of euthanasia would appear again. The accuracy of their prediction was undeniable. What is more interesting, however, is how it was possible that there were no protests on the part of medical organizations when the bishops brought the program to the attention of the public. Not only did the euthanasia program contradict the passage in the Hippocratic oath that states, "I will not give any man a fatal poison, even if he asks me for it," but further, since there was no legal measure assuring the impunity of euthanasia, the physicians who participated in the program could have found themselves in a delicate legal situation (this last circumstance did give rise to protests on the part of jurists and lawyers). The fact is that the National Socialist Reich marks the point at which the integration of medicine and politics, which is one of the essential characteristics of modern biopolitics, began to assume its final form. This implies that the sovereign decision on bare life comes to be displaced from strictly political motivations and areas to a more ambiguous terrain in which the physician and the sovereign seem to exchange roles.

§ 4 'Politics, or Giving Form to the Life of a People'

4.1. In 1942, the Institut allemand in Paris decided to circulate a publication designed to inform French friends and allies of the character and merits of National Socialist politics in matters of health and eugenics. The book, which is a collection of statements by the most authoritative German specialists in these areas (such as Eugen Fischer and Ottmar von Verschuer), as well as other figures responsible for the medical politics of the Reich (such as Libero Conti and Hans Reiter), bears the significant title *State and Health* (*État et santé*). Of all the official or semiofficial publications of the National Socialist regime, this work perhaps most explicitly thematizes the politicization (or political value) of biological life and the consequent transformation of the entire political horizon. "In the centuries that came before us," Reiter writes,

> large conflicts between peoples were more or less caused by the necessity of guaranteeing the possessions of the State (by "possessions," we mean not only the country's territory but also its material contents). The threat that neighboring States might expand territorially has thus often been the cause of conflicts in which individuals, considered so to speak as means to achieve the desired goals, were ignored.
>
> Only in Germany at the beginning of our century, starting with distinctly liberal theories, was the value of men finally taken into account and defined, if in a manner that was of course grounded on the liberal forms and principles that dominated the economy. . . .

144

While Helferich estimated German national assets at about three hundred and ten million marks, Zahn thus observed that in addition to this material wealth, there is also a "living wealth" worth one thousand and sixty-one million marks. (in Verschuer, *État et santé,* p. 31)

According to Reiter, the great novelty of National Socialism lies in the fact that this living wealth now enters the foreground of the Reich's interests and calculations, founding a new politics. This politics begins first of all with the establishment of a "budget to take account of the living value of people" (ibid., p. 34), and it proposes to assume the care of the "biological body of the nation" (ibid., p. 51): "We are approaching a logical synthesis of biology and economy. . . . Politics will more and more have to be capable of achieving this synthesis, which may only be in its first stages today, but which still allows one to recognize the interdependence of the forces of biology and economy as an inevitable fact" (ibid., p. 48).

Hence the radical transformation of the meaning and duties of medicine, which is increasingly integrated into the functions and the organs of the state: "Just as the economist and the merchant are responsible for the economy of material values, so the physician is responsible for the economy of human values. . . . It is absolutely necessary that the physician contribute to a rationalized human economy, that he recognize that the level of the people's health is the condition for economic gain. . . . Fluctuations in the biological substance and in the material budget are usually parallel" (ibid., p. 40).

The principles of this new biopolitics are dictated by eugenics, which is understood as the science of a people's genetic heredity. Foucault has documented the increasing importance that the science of police assumes starting in the eighteenth century, when, with Nicolas De Lemare, Johan Peter Franc, and J. H. G. von Justi, it takes as its explicit objective the total care of the population (*Dits et écrits,* 4: 150–61). From the end of the nineteenth century, Francis Galton's work functions as the theoretical background for the work of the science of police, which has by now become biopolitics. It is important to observe that Nazism, contrary to a common prejudice, did not limit itself to using and twisting scien-

tific concepts for its own ends. The relationship between National
Socialist ideology and the social and biological sciences of the
time—in particular, genetics—is more intimate and complex and,
at the same time, more disturbing. A glance at the contributions of
Verschuer (who, surprising as this may seem, continued to teach
genetics and anthropology at the University of Frankfurt even after
the fall of the Third Reich) and Fischer (the director of the Kaiser
Wilhelm Institute for Anthropology in Berlin) shows beyond a
doubt that the genetic research of the time, which had recently discovered the localization of genes in chromosomes (those genes that
"are ordered," as Fischer writes, "like pearls in a necklace"), gave
National Socialist biopolitics its fundamental conceptual structure.
"Race," Fischer writes, "is not determined by the assembly of this
or that measurable characteristic, as in the case, for example, of a
scale of colors. . . . Race is genetic heredity and nothing but
heredity" (in Verschuer, *État et santé*, p. 84). It is not surprising,
therefore, that the exemplary reference studies for both Verschuer
and Fischer are T. H. Morgan and J. B. S. Haldane's experiments
on drosophila and, more generally, the very same works of Anglo-
Saxon genetics that led, during the same years, to the formation of
the first map of the X chromosome in man and the first certain
identification of hereditary pathological predispositions.

The new fact, however, is that these concepts are not treated as
external (if binding) criteria of a sovereign decision: they are,
rather, as such immediately political. Thus the concept of race is
defined, in accordance with the genetic theories of the age, as "a
group of human beings who manifest a certain combination of
homozygotic genes that are lacking in other groups" (Verschuer,
État et santé, p. 88). Yet both Fischer and Verschuer know that a
pure race is, according to this definition, almost impossible to
identify (in particular, neither the Jews nor the Germans constitute
a race in the strict sense—and Hitler is just as aware of this when he
writes *Mein Kampf* as when he decides on the Final Solution).
"Racism" (if one understands race to be a strictly biological concept) is, therefore, not the most correct term for the biopolitics of
the Third Reich. National Socialist biopolitics moves, instead, in a

horizon in which the "care of life" inherited from eighteenth-century police science is, in now being founded on properly eugenic concerns, absolutized. Distinguishing between politics (*Politik*) and police (*Polizei*), von Justi assigned the first a merely negative task, the fight against the external and internal enemies of the State, and the second a positive one, the care and growth of the citizens' life. National Socialist biopolitics—and along with it, a good part of modern politics even outside the Third Reich—cannot be grasped if it is not understood as necessarily implying the disappearance of the difference between the two terms: the *police* now becomes *politics*, and the care of life coincides with the fight against the enemy. "The National Socialist revolution," one reads in the introduction to *State and Health*, "wishes to appeal to forces that want to exclude factors of biological degeneration and to maintain the people's hereditary health. It thus aims to fortify the health of the people as a whole and to eliminate influences that harm the biological growth of the nation. The book does not discuss problems that concern only one people; it brings out problems of vital importance for all European civilization." Only from this perspective is it possible to grasp the full sense of the extermination of the Jews, in which the police and politics, eugenic motives and ideological motives, the care of health and the fight against the enemy become absolutely indistinguishable.

4.2. A few years earlier, Verschuer had published a booklet in which National Socialist ideology finds what may well be its most rigorous biopolitical formulation: " 'The new State knows no other task than the fulfillment of the conditions necessary for the preservation of the people.' These words of the Führer mean that every political act of the National Socialist state serves the life of the people. . . . We know today that the life of the people is only secured if the racial traits and hereditary health of the body of the people [*Volkskörper*] are preserved" (*Rassenhygiene*, p. 5).

The link between politics and life instituted by these words is not (as is maintained by a common and completely inadequate interpretation of racism) a merely instrumental relationship, as if race were a simple natural given that had merely to be safeguarded. *The novelty of modern biopolitics lies in the fact that the biological given is as such immediately political, and the political is as such immediately the biological given.* "Politics," Verschuer writes, "that is, giving form to the life of the people [*Politik, das heißt die Gestaltung des Lebens des Volkes*]" (*Rassenhygiene*, p. 8). The life that, with the declarations of rights, became the ground of sovereignty now becomes the subject-object of state politics (which therefore appears more and more in the form of "police"). But only a state essentially founded on the very life of the nation could identify its own principal vocation as the formation and care of the "body of the people."

Hence the seeming contradiction according to which a *natural given* tends to present itself as a *political task.* "Biological heredity," Verschuer continues, "is certainly a destiny, and accordingly, we prove ourselves masters of this destiny insofar as we take biological heredity to be the task that has been assigned to us and which we must fulfill." The paradox of Nazi biopolitics and the necessity by which it was bound to submit life itself to an incessant political mobilization could not be expressed better than by this transformation of natural heredity into a political task. *The totalitarianism of our century has its ground in this dynamic identity of life and politics, without which it remains incomprehensible.* If Nazism still appears to us as an enigma, and if its affinity with Stalinism (on which Hannah Arendt so much insisted) is still unexplained, this is because we have failed to situate the totalitarian phenomenon in its entirety in the horizon of biopolitics. When life and politics—originally divided, and linked together by means of the no-man's-land of the state of exception that is inhabited by bare life—begin to become one, all life becomes sacred and all politics becomes the exception.

4.3. Only from this perspective can one understand why precisely the laws concerning eugenics were among the first issued by the National Socialist regime. On July 14, 1933, a few weeks after Hitler's rise to power, the law for the "prevention of the continuance of hereditary disease" was promulgated, stipulating that "those afflicted with a hereditary disease may be sterilized by a surgical operation if there is medical evidence to suggest that their descendants will most likely be afflicted by serious hereditary disorders of the body or the mind." On October 18, 1933, eugenic legislation was extended to marriage by the law for the "protection of the hereditary health of the German people," which stated:

> No marriage may be performed (1) when one of the betrothed suffers from a contagious disease that might seriously threaten the spouse or any descendants; (2) when one of the betrothed is debarred or temporarily a ward; (3) when one of the betrothed, while not a ward, suffers from a mental illness that might make the marriage seem undesirable for the national community; (4) when one of the betrothed suffers from one of the hereditary diseases provided for by the law of July 14, 1933.

The sense of these laws and the rapidity with which they were issued cannot be grasped as long as they are confined to the domain of eugenics. What is decisive is that for the Nazis these laws had an immediately political character. As such, they are inseparable from the Nuremberg laws on "citizenship in the Reich" and on the "protection of German blood and honor," which transformed Jews into second-class citizens, forbidding, among other things, marriage between Jews and full citizens and also stipulating that even citizens of Aryan blood had to prove themselves worthy of German honor (which allowed the possibility of denationalization to hang implicitly over everyone). The laws authorizing discrimination against the Jews have almost completely monopolized scholarly interest in the racial politics of the Third Reich. And yet the laws concerning the Jews can only be fully understood if they are brought back to the general context of National Socialism's legislation and biopolitical praxis. This legislation and this praxis are not simply reducible to the Nuremberg laws, to the deportations to the camps, or even to the "Final Solution": these decisive events of our century have their foundation in the unconditional assumption of a biopolitical task in which life and politics become one ("Politics, that is, giving form to the life of the people"). Only when these events are brought back to their "humanitarian" context can their inhumanity be measured.

When its biopolitical program showed its thanatopolitical face, the Nazi Reich was determined to extend itself over all citizens. Nothing proves this better than one of the projects proposed by Hitler in the last years of the war: "After national X-ray examination, the Fuehrer is to be given a list of sick persons, particularly those with lung and heart diseases. On the basis of the new Reich Health Law . . . these families will no longer be able to remain among the public and can no longer be allowed to produce children. What will happen to these families will be the subject of further orders of the Fuehrer" (quoted in Arendt, *Origins*, p. 416).

א Precisely this immediate unity of politics and life makes it possible to shed light on the scandal of twentieth-century philosophy: the relation between Martin Heidegger and Nazism. Only when situated in the perspective of modern biopolitics does this relation acquire its proper significance (and this is the very thing that both Heidegger's accusers and his defenders fail to do). The great novelty of Heidegger's thought (which did not elude the most attentive observers at Davos, such as Franz Rosenzweig and Emmanuel Levinas) was that it resolutely took root in facticity. As the publication of the lecture courses from the early 1920s has by now shown, ontology appears in Heidegger from the very beginning as a hermeneutics of factical life (*faktisches Leben*). The circular structure by which Dasein is an issue for itself in its ways of being is nothing but a formalization of the essential experience of factical life, in which it is impossible to distinguish between life and its actual situation, Being and its ways of Being, and for which all the distinctions of traditional anthropology (such as those between spirit and body, sensation and consciousness, I and world, subject and properties) are abolished. For Heidegger, the central category of facticity is not (as it was for Edmund Husserl) *Zufälligkeit*, contingency—by which one thing is in a certain way and in a certain place, yet could be elsewhere and otherwise—but rather *Verfallenheit*, fallenness, which characterizes a being that is and has to be its own ways of Being. Facticity does not mean simply being contingently in a certain way and a certain situation, but rather means decisively assuming this way and this situation by which what was given [*ciò che era dote*] (*Hingabe*) must be transformed into a task (*Aufgabe*). Dasein, the Being-there who is its There, thus comes to be placed in a zone of indiscernability with respect to—and to mark the definitive collapse of—all traditional determinations of man.

In a text of 1934 that may well even today still constitute the most valuable contribution to an understanding of National Socialism, Levinas proves himself the first to underline the analogies between this new ontological determination of man and certain traits of the philosophy implicit in Hitlerism. Judeo-Christian and liberal thought, according to Levinas, strive for the spirit's ascetic liberation from the bonds of the sensuous and historico-social situation into which it finds itself thrown, thus ultimately differentiating, in man and his world, between a realm of reason and a realm of the body, to which the realm of reason is irreducibly opposed. Hitler's philosophy (in this respect similar to Marxism) is instead, Levinas argues, founded on an absolutely unconditional assumption of the historical, physical, and material situation, which is considered as an indissoluble cohesion of spirit and body and nature and culture.

The body is not only a happy or unhappy accident that relates us to the implacable world of matter. Its adherence to the Self is of value in itself. It is an adherence that one does not escape and that no metaphor can confuse with the presence of an external object; it is a union that does not in any way alter the tragic character of finality. This feeling of identity between self and body . . . will therefore never allow those who wish to begin with it to rediscover, in the depths of this unity, the duality of a free spirit that struggles against the body to which it is chained. On the contrary, for such people, the whole of the spirit's essence lies in the fact that it is chained to the body. To separate the spirit from the concrete forms with which it is already involved is to betray the originality of the very feeling from which it is appropriate to begin. The importance attributed to this feeling for the body, with which the Western spirit has never wished to content itself, is at the basis of a new conception of man. The biological, with the notion of inevitability it entails, becomes more than an object of spiritual life. It becomes its heart. The mysterious urgings of the blood, the appeals of heredity and the past for which the body serves as an enigmatic vehicle, lose the character of being problems that are subject to a solution put forward by a sovereignly free Self. Not only does the Self bring in the unknown elements of these problems in order to resolve them; the Self is also

constituted by these elements. Man's essence lies no longer in freedom
but in a kind of bondage. . . . Chained to his body, man sees himself re-
fusing the power to escape from himself. Truth is no longer for him the
contemplation of a foreign spectacle; instead it consists in a drama in
which man is himself the actor. It is under the weight of his whole existence, which includes facts on which there is no going back, that man
will say his yes or his no. ("Quelques réflexions" [1934], pp. 205–7)

Though Levinas's text was written at a time when his teacher's support
of Nazism was still searing, the name Heidegger appears nowhere. But
the note added at the time of the text's republication in *Critical Inquiry* in
1990 leaves no doubt as to the thesis that an attentive reader would
nonetheless have had to read between the lines—namely, that Nazism as
an "elemental evil" has its condition of possibility in Western philosophy
itself, and in Heideggerian ontology in particular: "a possibility that is
inscribed in the ontology of Being's care for Being—for the being *dem es
in seinem Sein um dieses Sein selbst geht* ['for whom Being itself is an issue
in its being']" ("Reflections on the Philosophy of Hitlerism," p. 62).

There could be no clearer statement that Nazism is rooted in the same
experience of facticity from which Heidegger departs, and which the
philosopher had summarized in his *Rectoral Address* in the formula "to
will or not to will one's own Dasein." Only this essential proximity can
explain how Heidegger could have written the following revealing words
in his 1935 course, *Introduction to Metaphysics*: "The works that are being
peddled about nowadays as the philosophy of National Socialism have
nothing whatever to do with the inner truth and greatness of this
movement (namely the encounter between global technology and modern man); these works have all been written by men fishing in the
troubled waters of 'values' and 'totalities' " (*Einführung*, p. 152).

From Heidegger's perspective, National Socialism's error and betrayal
of its "inner truth" consists in its having transformed the experience of
factical life into a biological "value" (hence the contempt with which
Heidegger repeatedly refers to Rosenberg). While the greatest achievement of Heidegger's philosophical genius was to have elaborated the
conceptual categories that kept *facticity* from presenting itself as a *fact*,
Nazism ended with the incarceration of factical life in an objective racial
determination and, therefore, with the abandonment of its original
inspiration.

Yet what, beyond these differences and from the perspective that interests us, is the political meaning of the experience of facticity? For both Heidegger and National Socialism, life has no need to assume "values" external to it in order to become politics: life is immediately political in its very facticity. Man is not a living being who must abolish or transcend himself in order to become human—man is not a duality of spirit and body, nature and politics, life and *logos*, but is instead resolutely situated at the point of their indistinction. Man is no longer the "anthropophorous" animal who must transcend himself to give way to the human being; man's factical essence already contains the movement that, if grasped, constitutes him as Dasein and, therefore, as a political being ("*polis* signifies the place, the *Da*, where and how Dasein is insofar as Dasein is historical" [*Einführung*, p. 117]). This means, however, that the experience of facticity is equivalent to a radicalization without precedent of the state of exception (with its indistinction of nature and politics, outside and inside, exclusion and inclusion) in a dimension in which the state of exception tends to becomes the rule. It is as if the bare life of *homo sacer*, whose exclusion founded sovereign power, now became—in assuming itself as a task—explicitly and immediately political. And yet this is precisely what characterizes the biopolitical turn of modernity, that is, the condition in which we still find ourselves. And this is the point at which Nazism and Heidegger's thought radically diverge. Nazism determines the bare life of *homo sacer* in a biological and eugenic key, making it into the site of an incessant decision on value and nonvalue in which biopolitics continually turns into thanatopolitics and in which the camp, consequently, becomes the absolute political space. In Heidegger, on the other hand, *homo sacer*—whose very own life is always at issue in its every act—instead becomes Dasein, the inseparable unity of Being and ways of Being, of subject and qualities, life and world, "whose own Being is at issue in its very Being." If life, in modern biopolitics, is immediately politics, here this unity, which itself has the form of an irrevocable decision, withdraws from every external decision and appears as an indissoluble cohesion in which it is impossible to isolate something like a bare life. In the state of exception become the rule, the life of *homo sacer*, which was the correlate of sovereign power, turns into an existence over which power no longer seems to have any hold.

§ 5 VP

5.1. On May 15, 1941, Dr. Roscher, who for some time had been conducting experiments on rescue operations from high altitudes, wrote to Himmler. He asked whether, considering the importance of his research for the lives of German pilots, the mortal risk his experiments constituted for VPs (*Versuchspersonen*, human guinea pigs) and the fact that nothing of use could be gained from conducting experiments on animals, it might be possible to provide him with "two or three professional criminals" for his work. By this point the air war had already entered the stage of high-altitude flying, and the risk of death would be great if, under these conditions, the pressurized cabin were damaged or the pilot had to parachute from the plane. The final result of the exchange of letters between Roscher and Himmler (which is preserved in its entirety) was the installation at Dachau of a compression chamber to continue the experiments in a place in which VPs were particularly easy to find. We still possess the records (furnished with photographs) of the experiment conducted on a 37-year-old Jewish VP in good heath who was subjected to the equivalent pressure of 12,000 meters of altitude. "After four minutes," we read, "the VP began to sweat and to shake her head. After five minutes cramps were produced; between six and ten minutes breathing accelerated and the VP lost consciousness; between ten and thirty minutes breathing slowed down to three breaths a minute, and then ceased altogether. At the same time skin color became strongly cyanotic and foam appeared around the lips." Then follows the report of the dissection conducted to ascertain any possible organic lesions on the corpse.

At the Nuremberg trials, the experiments conducted by German physicians and scientists in the concentration camps were universally taken to be one of the most infamous chapters in the history of the National Socialist regime. In addition to experiments pertaining to high-altitude rescue operations, experiments were also conducted at Dachau on the possibility of survival in ice-cold water and on the potability of salt water (these experiments, too, were designed to facilitate the rescue of sailors and pilots who had fallen into the ocean). In the cold-water experiments, VPs were held under cold water until they lost consciousness, while researchers carefully analyzed the variations in body temperature and possibilities of reanimation. Particularly grotesque was the experiment on so-called animal heat reanimation, in which VPs were placed in a cot between two naked women who had also been taken from among the Jews detained in the camps; the documentation tells of a VP who was able to have sexual relations, which facilitated the recuperation process. The experiments on the potability of salt water were instead conducted on VPs chosen from among the prisoners bearing the black triangle (i.e., Gypsies; this symbol of the genocide of a defenseless population ought to be remembered alongside the yellow star). These VPs were divided into three groups: one that simply had to abstain from drinking altogether; one that drank only salt water; and one that drank salt water mixed with *Berkazusatz*, a chemical substance that, according to the researchers, lessened the harm of the salt water.

Another important area of experimentation involved inoculation with petechial fever bacteria and the *Hepatitis endemica* virus in the hope of producing vaccines against two infectious diseases that were especially threatening to the health of German soldiers on the battlefronts, where life was hardest. Experimentation on nonsurgical sterilization by means of chemical substances or radiation, which was to serve the Reich's eugenic politics, was, in

156 The Camp as Paradigm

addition, particularly severe and painful for subjects. Less often, experiments were also conducted on limb transplants, cellular inflammations, and so on.

5.2. Reading the testimony of VPs who survived, in some cases the testimony of the very subjects described in the extant records, is such an atrocious experience that it is very tempting to consider the experiments as merely sadocriminal acts with no relation to scientific research. But unfortunately this cannot be done. To begin with, some (certainly not all) of the physicians who conducted the experiments were quite well respected by the scientific community for their research. Professor Clauberg, for example, who was responsible for the sterilization program, was the inventor of the "Clauberg test" on progesterone action, which was commonly used in gynecology until a few years ago. Professors Schröder, Becker-Freyting, and Bergblöck, who directed the experiments on the potability of salt water, enjoyed such a good scientific reputation that after they were convicted, a group of scientists from various countries submitted a petition to an international congress of medicine in 1948 so that these scientists "might not be confused with other criminal physicians sentenced in Nuremberg." And during their trial, Professor Vollardt, a professor of chemistry at the University of Frankfurt, who was not considered to have sympathies for the Nazi regime, testified before the court that "from the scientific point of view, the preparation of these experiments was splendid"—a curious adjective, if one considers that the VPs reached such a level of prostration in the course of the experiment that they twice tried to suck fresh water from a rag on the floor.

What is decisively more disquieting is the fact (which is unequivocally shown by the scientific literature put forward by the defense and confirmed by the expert witnesses appointed by the court) that experiments on prisoners and persons sentenced to death had been performed several times and on a large scale in our century, in particular in the United States (the very country from which most of the Nuremberg judges came). Thus in the 1920s, 800 people held in United States prisons were infected with malaria plasmodia in an attempt to find an antidote to paludism. There were also the experiments—widely held to be exemplary in the scientific literature on pellagra—conducted by Goldberg on twelve prisoners sentenced to death, who were promised the remission of their penalty if they survived experimentation. Outside the United States, the first experiments with cultures of the beriberi bacillus were conducted by R. P. Strong in Manila on persons sentenced to death (the records of the experiment do not mention whether participation in the experiment was voluntary). In addition, the defense cited the case of Keanu (Hawaii), who was infected with leprosy in order to be promised pardon, and who died following the experiment.

Confronted with this documentation, the judges were forced to dedicate interminable discussions to the identification of criteria that might render scientific experiments on human guinea pigs admissible. The final criterion, which elicited general agreement, was the necessity of an explicit and voluntary consent on the part of the subject who was to be submitted to the experiment. The consistent practice in the United States was (as shown by a form in use in the state of Illinois which was displayed before the judges) to have the sentenced person sign a declaration in which the following, among other things, is stated:

> I assume all the risks of this experiment and declare that I absolve the University of Chicago and all the technicians and researchers who take part in the experiment, as well as the government of Illinois, the directory of the State penitentiary and every other official, even as concerns my heirs and representatives, of any responsibility. I therefore renounce every claim to any damage or disease, even fatal, which may be caused by the experiment.

The obvious hypocrisy of such documents cannot fail to leave one perplexed. To speak of free will and consent in the case of a person sentenced to death or of a detained person who must pay serious penalties is, at the very least, questionable. And it is certain that even if similar declarations had been signed by the people detained in the camps, the experiments that took place would not have been considered ethically admissible. What the well-meaning

emphasis on the free will of the individual refuses to recognize here
is that the concept of "voluntary consent" is simply meaningless for
someone interned at Dachau, even if he or she is promised an
improvement in living conditions. From this point of view, the
inhumanity of the experiments in the United States and in the
camps is, therefore, substantially equivalent.

Nor was it possible to invoke a difference of ends in order to
evaluate the different and specific responsibilities in the cases at
issue. An observation by Alexander Mitscherlich, the doctor who,
together with F. Mielke, published the first account of the physicians' trials in Nuremberg in 1947, bears witness to the difficulty of
admitting that the experiments in the camps were not without
medico-scientific precedent. When Professor Rose was tried for
experiments with vaccination against petechial fever (which had
brought death to 97 of 392 VPs), he defended himself by citing the
analogous experiments conducted by Strong in Manila on persons
sentenced to death. Rose compared the German soldiers who died
of petechial fever to the people with beriberi for whose benefit
Strong's research was intended. At this point Mitscherlich, who
otherwise distinguishes himself by the sobriety of his comments,
objects: "While Strong was trying to fight against the misery and
death caused by a scourge of the natural order, researchers like the
accused Professor Rose worked, in the confusion of a dictatorship's
inhuman methods, to maintain and justify cruelty" (Mitscherlich
and Mielke, *Wissenschaft*, pp. 11–12). As a historico-political judgment, the observation is exact. It is clear, however, that the ethico-
juridical admissibility of the experiments could not in any way
depend on either the nationality of the people for whom the
vaccine was destined or the circumstances in which they had
contracted the disease.

The only ethically correct position would have been to recognize
that the precedents cited by the defense were pertinent, but that
they did not diminish the responsibility of the accused in the
slightest. But this would have meant throwing a sinister shadow on
common practices of the medical profession. (Since the time of the
trial, even more sensational cases of mass experiments conducted

on citizens have come to light, for example, in the study of the effects of nuclear radiation.) If it was theoretically comprehensible that such experiments would not raise ethical problems for officials and researchers inside a totalitarian regime that moved in an openly biopolitical horizon, how could experiments that were, in a certain sense, analogous have been conducted in a democratic country?

The only possible answer is that in both contexts the particular status of the VPs was decisive; they were persons sentenced to death or detained in a camp, the entry into which meant the definitive exclusion from the political community. Precisely because they were lacking almost all the rights and expectations that we customarily attribute to human existence, and yet were still biologically alive, they came to be situated in a limit zone between life and death, inside and outside, in which they were no longer anything but bare life. Those who are sentenced to death and those who dwelt in the camps are thus in some way unconsciously assimilated to *homines sacres*, to a life that may be killed without the commission of homicide. Like the fence of the camp, the interval between death sentence and execution delimits an extratemporal and extraterritorial threshold in which the human body is separated from its normal political status and abandoned, in a state of exception, to the most extreme misfortunes. In such a space of exception, subjection to experimentation can, like an expiation rite, either return the human body to life (pardon and the remission of a penalty are, it is worth remembering, manifestations of the sovereign power over life and death) or definitively consign it to the death to which it already belongs. What concerns us most of all here, however, is that in the biopolitical horizon that characterizes modernity, the physician and the scientist move in the no-man's-land into which at one point the sovereign alone could penetrate.

§ 6 Politicizing Death

6.1. In 1959, P. Mollaret and M. Goulon, two French neuro-physiologists, published a brief study in the *Revue neurologique* in which they added the new and extreme figure of what they called *coma dépassé* ("overcoma," it could be rendered) to the known phenomenology of the coma. In addition to the classical coma, which is characterized by the loss of relational life functions (consciousness, mobility, sensibility, reflexes), the medical literature of the time also distinguished an alert coma, in which the loss of relational functions was not complete, and a *carus* coma, in which the preservation of vegetative life functions was seriously threatened. "To these three traditional degrees of coma," Mollaret and Goulon provocatively wrote, "we would like to add a fourth degree, *coma dépassé* . . . , i.e., a coma in which the total abolition of relational life functions corresponds to an equally total abolition of vegetative life functions" ("Le coma dépassé," p. 4).

The deliberately paradoxical formulation—a stage of life beyond the cessation of all vital functions—suggests that overcoma is the full fruit (the *rançon*, the authors call it, using the term that indicates the ransom or excessive price paid for something) of new life-support technology: artificial respiration, maintenance of cardiac circulation through intravenous perfusion of adrenaline, technologies of body temperature control, and so on. The survival of the overcomatose person automatically ended as soon as the life-support system was interrupted: the complete absence of any reaction to stimuli characteristic of deep coma was followed by immediate cardiovascular collapse and the cessation of all respiratory movement. Yet if life support continued, survival could be prolonged to the point at which the myocardium, by now independent of all afferent nerves, was once again capable of contracting with a rhythm and an energy sufficient to assure the vascularization of the other visceral arteries (normally not for more than a few days). But was this really "survival"? What was the zone of life beyond coma? Who or what is the overcomatose person? "Confronted with the unfortunate people who embody the state we have defined with the term *coma dépassé*," the authors write, "when the heart continues to beat day after day without producing even the smallest revival of life functions, desperation finally wins out over pity, and the temptation to push the liberating interruption button grows piercing" ("Le coma dépassé," p. 14).

6.2. Mollaret and Goulon immediately realized that the significance of *coma dépassé* far exceeded the technico-scientific problem of resuscitation: at stake was nothing less than a redefinition of death. Until then, the task of determining death was given over to the physician, who made use of the traditional criteria that had remained substantially the same throughout the centuries: the stopping of the heartbeat and the cessation of breathing. Overcoma rendered obsolete precisely these two ancient categories for the assessment of death and, opening a no-man's-land between coma and death, made it necessary to identify new criteria and establish new definitions. As the two neurophysiologists wrote, the problem expands "to the point of putting the final borders of life in question, and even further, to the determination of a right to establish the hour of legal death" ("Le coma dépassé," p. 4).

The problem became even more urgent and complicated by virtue of a historical coincidence that was perhaps accidental: the progress of life-support technology that made the *coma dépassé* possible occurred at the very same time as the development and refinement of transplant technologies. The state of the overcomatose person was the ideal condition for the removal of organs, but an exact definition of the moment of death was required in order for the surgeon responsible for the transplant not to be liable for homicide. In 1968, the report of a special Harvard University committee ("The *Ad Hoc* Committee of the Harvard Medical School") determined new criteria of death and inaugurated the concept of "brain death," which was to impress itself more and more (if not without lively opposition) upon the international scientific community, until it finally penetrated the legislation of many American and European states. The dark zone beyond coma, which Mollaret and Goulon had left wavering uncertainly between life and death, now furnishes precisely the new criterion of death. ("Our first objective," the Harvard report begins, "is to define irreversible coma as a new criterion of death.")[1] Once adequate medical tests had confirmed the death of the entire brain (not only of the neocortex but also of the brain stem), the patient was to be considered dead, even if, thanks to life-support technology, he continued breathing.

6.3. Obviously it is not our intention to enter into the scientific debate on whether brain death constitutes a necessary and sufficient criterion for the declaration of death or whether the final word must be left to traditional criteria. It is impossible, however, to avoid the impression that the entire discussion is wrapped up in inextricable logical contradictions, and that the concept "death," far from having become more exact, now oscillates from one pole to the other with the greatest indeterminacy, describing a vicious circle that is truly exemplary. On the one hand, brain death is taken to be the only rigorous criterion of death and is, accordingly, substituted for systematic or somatic death, which is now considered to be insufficient. But on the other hand, systematic or somatic death is still, with more or less self-consciousness, called in to furnish the decisive criterion. It is, in other words, surprising

1. Harvard University Medical School, "A Definition of Irreversible Coma," p. 85. Cited hereafter as Harvard report.

that the champions of brain death can candidly write that brain death "inevitably leads quite quickly to death" (Walton, *Brain Death*, p. 51), or, as in the report of the Finnish Department of Health, that "these patients [who had been diagnosed as brain dead and who were, therefore, already dead] died within a day" (quoted in Lamb, *Death*, p. 56). David Lamb, an advocate of the concept of brain death who has himself noted these contradictions, writes the following, after citing a series of studies that show that heart failure comes within a few days of the diagnosis of brain death: "In most of these studies there are minor variations in the clinical tests, but all nevertheless demonstrated the inevitability of somatic death following brain death" (ibid., p. 63). According to a clear logical inconsistency, heart failure—which was just rejected as a valid criterion of death—reappears to prove the exactness of the criterion that is to substitute for it.

This wavering of death in a shadowy zone beyond coma is also reflected in an analogous oscillation between medicine and law, medical decision and legal decision. In 1974, Andrew D. Lyons's defense lawyer, whose client was accused before a California court of having killed a man with a gunshot, objected that the cause of the victim's death was not the bullet shot by his client but rather the surgeon Norman Shumway's removal of the brain-dead patient's heart for the sake of performing a transplant. Dr. Shumway was not charged, but one can only read with unease the declaration with which he convinced the court of his own innocence: "I'm saying anyone whose brain is dead is dead. It is the one determinant that would be universally applicable, because the brain is the one organ that can't be transplanted" (quoted in Lamb, *Death*, p. 75). According to any good logic, this would imply that just as heart failure no longer furnishes a valid criterion for death once life-support technology and transplantation are discovered, so brain death would, hypothetically speaking, cease to be death on the day on which the first brain transplant were performed. Death, in this way, becomes an epiphenomenon of transplant technology.

A perfect example of this wavering is the case of Karen Quinlan, the American girl who went into deep coma and was kept alive for years by means of artificial respiration and nutrition. On the request of her parents, a court finally allowed her artificial respiration to be interrupted on the grounds that the girl was to be considered as already dead. At that point Karen, while remaining in coma, began to breath naturally and "survived" in a state of artificial nutrition until 1985, the year of her natural "death." It is clear that Karen Quinlan's body had, in fact, entered a zone of indetermination in which the words "life" and "death" had lost their meaning, and which, at least in this sense, is not unlike the space of exception inhabited by bare life.

6.4. This means that today—as is implicit in Peter Medawar's observation that "in biology, discussions on the meaning of the words 'life' and 'death' are signs of a low level conversation"—life and death are not properly scientific concepts but rather political concepts, which as such acquire a political meaning precisely only through a decision. The "frightful and incessantly deferred borders" of which Mollaret and Goulon spoke are moving borders because they are *biopolitical* borders, and the fact that today a vast process is under way in which what is at stake is precisely the redefinition of these borders indicates that the exercise of sovereign power now passes through them more than ever and, once again, cuts across the medical and biological sciences.

In a brilliant article, W. Gaylin evokes the specter of bodies, which he calls "neomorts," which would have the legal status of corpses but would maintain some of the characteristics of life for the sake of possible future transplants: "They would be warm, pulsating and urinating" ("Harvesting," p. 30). In an opposite camp, the body kept alive by life-support systems has been defined by a supporter of brain death as a *faux vivant* on which it is permitted to intervene without any reservations (Dagognet, *La maîtrise*, p. 189).

The hospital room in which the neomort, the overcomatose person, and the *faux vivant* waver between life and death delimits a space of exception in which a purely bare life, entirely controlled by man and his technology, appears for the first time. And since it is precisely a question not of a natural life but of an extreme embodiment of *homo sacer* (the comatose person has been defined as an intermediary being between man and an animal), what is at stake is, once again, the definition of a life that may be killed without the commission of homicide (and that is, like *homo sacer*, "unsacrificeable," in the sense that it obviously could not be put to death following a death sentence).

This is why it is not surprising that some of the most ardent partisans of brain death and modern biopolitics propose that the state should decide on the moment of death, removing all obstacles to intervention on the *faux vivant*.

> We must therefore define the moment of the end and not rely on the rigidification of the corpse, as was done at one point, or, even less, on signs of putrefaction, but rather simply keep to brain death. . . . What follows from this is the possibility of intervening on the *faux vivant*. Only the State can do this and must do this. . . . Organisms belong to the public power: the body is nationalized [*les organismes appartiennent à la puissance publique: on nationalise le corps*]. (Dagognet, *La maîtrise*, p. 189).

Neither Reiter nor Verschuer had ever gone so far along the path of the politicization of bare life. But (and this is a clear sign that biopolitics has passed beyond a new threshold) in modern democracies it is possible to state in public what the Nazi biopoliticians did not dare to say.

§ 7 The Camp as the 'Nomos' of the Modern

7.1. What happened in the camps so exceeds the juridical concept of crime that the specific juridico-political structure in which those events took place is often simply omitted from consideration. The camp is merely the place in which the most absolute *conditio inhumana* that has ever existed on earth was realized: this is what counts in the last analysis, for the victims as for those who come after. Here we will deliberately follow an inverse line of inquiry. Instead of deducing the definition of the camp from the events that took place there, we will ask: What is a camp, what is its juridico-political structure, that such events could take place there? This will lead us to regard the camp not as a historical fact and an anomaly belonging to the past (even if still verifiable) but in some way as the hidden matrix and *nomos* of the political space in which we are still living.

Historians debate whether the first camps to appear were the *campos de concentraciones* created by the Spanish in Cuba in 1896 to suppress the popular insurrection of the colony, or the "concentration camps"[1] into which the English herded the Boers toward the start of the century. What matters here is that in both cases, a state of emergency linked to a colonial war is extended to an entire civil population. The camps are thus born not out of ordinary law (even

1. In English in the original.—Trans.

less, as one might have supposed, from a transformation and development of criminal law) but out of a state of exception and martial law. This is even clearer in the Nazi *Lager,* concerning whose origin and juridical regime we are well informed. It has been noted that the juridical basis for internment was not common law but *Schutzhaft* (literally, protective custody), a juridical institution of Prussian origin that the Nazi jurors sometimes classified as a preventative police measure insofar as it allowed individuals to be "taken into custody" independently of any criminal behavior, solely to avoid danger to the security of the state. The origin of *Schutzhaft* lies in the Prussian law of June 4, 1851, on the state of emergency, which was extended to all of Germany (with the exception of Bavaria) in 1871. An even earlier origin for *Schutzhaft* can be located in the Prussian laws on the "protection of personal liberty" (*Schutz der persönlichen Freiheit*) of February 12, 1850, which were widely applied during the First World War and during the disorder in Germany that followed the signing of the peace treaty. It is important not to forget that the first concentration camps in Germany were the work not of the Nazi regime but of the Social-Democratic governments, which interned thousands of communist militants in 1923 on the basis of *Schutzhaft* and also created the *Konzentrationslager für Ausländer* at Cottbus-Sielow, which housed mainly Eastern European refugees and which may, therefore, be considered the first camp for Jews in this century (even if it was, obviously, not an extermination camp).

The juridical foundation for *Schutzhaft* was the proclamation of the state of siege or of exception and the corresponding suspension of the articles of the German constitution that guaranteed personal liberties. Article 48 of the Weimar constitution read as follows: "The president of the Reich may, in the case of a grave disturbance or threat to public security and order, make the decisions necessary to reestablish public security, if necessary with the aid of the armed forces. To this end he may provisionally suspend [*ausser Kraft setzen*] the fundamental rights contained in articles 114, 115, 117, 118, 123, 124, and 153." From 1919 to 1924, the Weimar governments declared the state of exception many times, sometimes prolonging it for up to five months (for example, from September 1923 to February 1924). In this sense, when the Nazis took power and proclaimed the "decree for the protection of the people and State" (*Verordnung zum Schutz von Volk und Staat*) on February 28, 1933, indefinitely suspending the articles of the constitution concerning personal liberty, the freedom of expression and of assembly, and the inviolability of the home and of postal and telephone privacy, they merely followed a practice consolidated by previous governments.

Yet there was an important novelty. No mention at all was made of the expression *Ausnahmezustand* ("state of exception") in the text of the decree, which was, from the juridical point of view, implicitly grounded in article 48 of the constitution then in force, and which without a doubt amounted to a declaration of the state of exception ("articles 114, 115, 117, 118, 123, 124, and 153 of the constitution of the German Reich," the first paragraph read, "are suspended until further notice"). The decree remained de facto in force until the end of the Third Reich, which has in this sense been aptly defined as a "Night of St. Bartholomew that lasted twelve years" (Drobisch and Wieland, *System*, p. 26). *The state of exception thus ceases to be referred to as an external and provisional state of factual danger and comes to be confused with juridical rule itself.* National Socialist jurists were so aware of the particularity of the situation that they defined it by the paradoxical expression "state of willed exception" (*einen gewollten Ausnahmezustand*). "Through the suspension of fundamental rights," writes Werner Spohr, a jurist close to the regime, "the decree brings into being a state of willed exception for the sake of the establishment of the National Socialist State" (quoted ibid., p. 28).

7.2. The importance of this constitutive nexus between the state of exception and the concentration camp cannot be overestimated for a correct understanding of the nature of the camp. The "protection" of freedom that is at issue in *Schutzhaft* is, ironically, protection against the suspension of law that characterizes the emergency. The novelty is that *Schutzhaft* is now separated from the state of exception on which it had been based and is left in force in the normal situation. *The camp is the space that is opened when the state of exception begins to become the rule.* In the camp, the state of exception, which was essentially a temporary suspension of the rule of law on the basis of a factual state of danger, is now given a permanent spatial arrangement, which as such nevertheless remains outside the normal order. When Himmler decided to create a "concentration camp for political prisoners" in Dachau at the time of Hitler's election as chancellor of the Reich in March 1933, the camp was immediately entrusted to the SS and—thanks to *Schutzhaft*—placed outside the rules of penal and prison law, which then and subsequently had no bearing on it. Despite the multiplication of the often contradictory communiqués, instructions, and telegrams through which the authorities both of the Reich and of the individual *Länder* took care to keep the workings of *Schutzhaft* as vague as possible after the decree of February 28, the camp's absolute independence from every judicial control and every reference to the normal juridical order was constantly reaffirmed. According to the new notions of the National Socialist jurists (among whom Carl Schmitt was in the front lines), which located the primary and immediate source of law in the Führer's command, *Schutzhaft* had, moreover, no need whatsoever of a juridical foundation in existing institutions and laws, being "an immediate effect of the National Socialist revolution" (Drobisch and Wieland, *System*, p. 27). Because of this—that is, insofar as the camps were located in such a peculiar space of exception—Diels, the head of the Gestapo, could declare, "Neither an order nor an instruction exists for the origin of the camps: they were not instituted; one day they were there [*sie waren nicht gegründet, sie waren eines Tages da*]" (quoted ibid., p. 30).

Dachau and the other camps that were immediately added to it (Sachsenhausen, Buchenwald, Lichtenberg) remained almost always in operation—what varied was the size of their population (which in certain periods, in particular between 1935 and 1937, before the Jews began to be deported, diminished to 7,500 people). But in Germany the camp as such had become a permanent reality.

7.3. The paradoxical status of the camp as a space of exception must be considered. The camp is a piece of land placed outside the normal juridical order, but it is nevertheless not simply an external space. What is excluded in the camp is, according to the etymological sense of the term "exception" (*ex-capere*), *taken outside*, included through its own exclusion. But what is first of all taken into the juridical order is the state of exception itself. Insofar as the state of exception is "willed," it inaugurates a new juridico-political paradigm in which the norm becomes indistinguishable from the exception. The camp is thus the structure in which the state of exception—the possibility of deciding on which founds sovereign power—is realized *normally*. The sovereign no longer limits himself, as he did in the spirit of the Weimar constitution, to deciding on the exception on the basis of recognizing a given factual situation (danger to public safety): laying bare the inner structure of the ban that characterizes his power, he now de facto produces the situation as a consequence of his decision on the exception. This is why in the camp the *quaestio iuris* is, if we look carefully, no longer strictly distinguishable from the *quaestio facti*, and in this sense every question concerning the legality or illegality of what happened there simply makes no sense. *The camp is a hybrid of law and fact in which the two terms have become indistinguishable.*

Hannah Arendt once observed that in the camps, the principle that supports totalitarian rule and that common sense obstinately refuses to admit comes fully to light: this is the principle according to which "everything is possible." Only because the camps constitute a space of exception in the sense we have examined—in which not only is law completely suspended but fact and law are completely confused—is everything in the camps truly possible. If this particular juridico-political structure of the camps—the task of which is precisely to create a stable exception—is not understood, the incredible things that happened there remain completely unintelligible. Whoever entered the camp moved in a zone of indistinction between outside and inside, exception and rule, licit and illicit, in which the very concepts of subjective right and juridical protection no longer made any sense. What is more, if the person entering the camp was a Jew, he had already been deprived of his rights as a citizen by the Nuremberg laws and was subsequently completely denationalized at the time of the Final Solution. Insofar as its inhabitants were stripped of every political status and wholly reduced to bare life, the camp was also the most absolute biopolitical space ever to have been realized, in which power confronts nothing but pure life, without any mediation. This is why the camp is the very paradigm of political space at the point at which politics becomes biopolitics and *homo sacer* is virtually confused with the citizen. The correct question to pose concerning the horrors committed in the camps is, therefore, not the hypocritical one of how crimes of such atrocity could be committed against human beings. It would be more honest and, above all, more useful to investigate carefully the juridical procedures and deployments of power by which human beings could be so completely deprived of their rights and prerogatives that no act committed against them could appear any longer as a crime. (At this point, in fact, everything had truly become possible.)

7.4. The bare life into which the camp's inhabitants were transformed is not, however, an extrapolitical, natural fact that law must limit itself to confirming or recognizing. It is, rather, a threshold in which law constantly passes over into fact and fact into law, and in which the two planes become indistinguishable. It is impossible to grasp the specificity of the National Socialist concept of race—and, with it, the peculiar vagueness and inconsistency that characterize it—if one forgets that the *biopolitical body* that constitutes the new fundamental political subject is neither a *quaestio facti* (for example, the identification of a certain biological body) nor a *quaestio iuris* (the identification of a certain juridical rule to be applied), but rather the site of a sovereign political decision that operates in the absolute indistinction of fact and law.

No one expressed this peculiar nature of the new fundamental biopolitical categories more clearly than Schmitt, who, in the essay "State, Movement, People," approximates the concept of race, without which "the National Socialist state could not exist, and without which its juridical life would not be possible," to the "general and indeterminate clauses" that had penetrated ever more deeply into German and European legislation in the twentieth century. In penetrating invasively into the juridical rule, Schmitt observes, concepts such as "good morals," "proper initiative," "important motive," "public security and order," "state of danger," and "case of necessity," which refer not to a rule but to a situation, rendered obsolete the illusion of a law that would a priori be able to regulate all cases and all situations and that judges would have to limit themselves simply to applying. In moving certainty and calculability outside the juridical rule, these clauses render all juridical concepts indeterminate. "In this sense," Schmitt writes, with unwittingly Kafkaesque accents,

> today there are now only 'indeterminate' juridical concepts. . . . The entire application of law thus lies between Scylla and Charybdis. The way forward seems to condemn us to a shoreless sea and to move us ever farther from the firm ground of juridical certainty and adherence to the law, which at the same time is still the ground of the judges' independence. Yet the way backward, which leads toward the formalistic superstition of law which was recognized as senseless and superseded long ago, is not worthy of consideration. (ibid., pp. 43–44)

A concept such as the National Socialist notion of race (or, in the words of Schmitt, of "equality of stock") functions as a general clause (analogous to "state of danger" or to "good morals") that does not refer to any situation of external fact but instead realizes an immediate coincidence of fact and law. The judge, the civil servant, or whoever else has to reckon with such a notion no longer orients himself according to a rule or a situation of fact. Binding himself solely to his own community of race with the German people and the Führer, such a person moves in a zone in which the distinction between life and politics, between questions of fact and questions of law, has literally no more meaning.

7.5. Only from this perspective does the National Socialist theory that posits the immediate and intrinsically perfect source of law in the word of the Führer acquire its full significance. Just as the word of the Führer is not a factual situation that is then transformed into a rule, but is rather itself rule insofar as it is living voice, so the biopolitical body (in its twofold appearance as Jewish body and German body, as life unworthy of being lived and as full life) is not an inert biological presupposition to which the rule refers, but at once rule and criterion of its own application, *a juridical rule that decides the fact that decides on its application.*

The radical novelty implicit in this conception has not been sufficiently noticed by historians of law. Not only is the law issued by the Führer definable neither as rule nor as exception and neither as law nor as fact. There is more: in this law, the formation of a rule [*normazione*] and the execution of a rule—the production of law and its application—are no longer distinguishable moments. (Benjamin understood this when he projected the Schmittian theory of sovereignty onto the baroque monarch, in whom "the gesture of execution" becomes constitutive and who, having to decide on the exception, is caught in the impossibility of making a decision [*Ursprung,* pp. 249–50].) The Führer is truly, according to the Pythagorean definition of the sovereign, a *nomos empsuchon,* a living law (Svenbro, *Phrasikleia,* p. 149). (This is why the separation of powers that characterizes the liberal-democratic State loses its meaning here, even if it remains formally in effect. Hence the difficulty of judging according to normal juridical criteria when judging those officials who, like Adolf Eichmann, did nothing other than execute the word of the Führer as law.)

This is the ultimate meaning of the Schmittian thesis that the principle of *Führung* is "a concept of the immediate present and of real presence" ("Staat," p. 42). And this is why Schmitt can affirm, without contradiction: "It is general knowledge among the contemporary German political generation that precisely the decision concerning whether a fact or a kind of thing is apolitical is a specifically political decision" (ibid., p. 17). Politics is now literally the decision concerning the unpolitical (that is, concerning bare life).

The camp is the space of this absolute impossibility of deciding between fact and law, rule and application, exception and rule, which nevertheless incessantly decides between them. What confronts the guard or the camp official is not an extrajuridical fact (an individual biologically belonging to the Jewish race) to which he must apply the discrimination of the National Socialist rule. On the contrary, every gesture, every event in the camp, from the most ordinary to the most exceptional, enacts the decision on bare life by which the German biopolitical body is made actual. The separation of the Jewish body is the immediate production of the specifically German body, just as its production is the application of the rule.

7.6. If this is true, if the essence of the camp consists in the materialization of the state of exception and in the subsequent creation of a space in which bare life and the juridical rule enter into a threshold of indistinction, then we must admit that we find ourselves virtually in the presence of a camp every time such a structure is created, independent of the kinds of crime that are committed there and whatever its denomination and specific topography. The stadium in Bari into which the Italian police in 1991 provisionally herded all illegal Albanian immigrants before sending them back to their country, the winter cycle-racing track in which the Vichy authorities gathered the Jews before consigning them to the Germans, the *Konzentrationslager für Ausländer* in Cottbus-Sielow in which the Weimar government gathered Jewish refugees from the East, or the *zones d'attentes* in French international airports in which foreigners asking for refugee status are detained will then all equally be camps. In all these cases, an apparently innocuous space (for example, the Hôtel Arcades in Roissy) actually delimits a space in which the normal order is de facto suspended and in which whether or not atrocities are committed depends not on law but on the civility and ethical sense of the police who temporarily act as sovereign (for example, in the four days during which foreigners can be held in the *zone d'attente* before the intervention of the judicial authority).

7.7. In this light, the birth of the camp in our time appears as an event that decisively signals the political space of modernity itself. It is produced at the point at which the political system of the modern nation-state, which was founded on the functional nexus between a determinate localization (land) and a determinate order (the State) and mediated by automatic rules for the inscription of life (birth or the nation), enters into a lasting crisis, and the State decides to assume directly the care of the nation's biological life as one of its proper tasks. If the structure of the nation-state is, in other words, defined by the three elements *land, order, birth*, the rupture of the old *nomos* is produced not in the two aspects that constituted it according to Schmitt (localization, *Ortung*, and order, *Ordnung*), but rather at the point marking the inscription of bare life (the *birth* that thus becomes *nation*) within the two of them. Something can no longer function within the traditional mechanisms that regulated this inscription, and the camp is the new, hidden regulator of the inscription of life in the order—or, rather, the sign of the system's inability to function without being transformed into a lethal machine. It is significant that the camps appear together with new laws on citizenship and the denationalization of citizens—not only the Nuremberg laws on citizenship in the Reich but also the laws on denationalization promulgated by almost all European states, including France, between 1915 and 1933. The state of exception, which was essentially a temporary suspension of the juridico-political order, now becomes a new and stable spatial arrangement inhabited by the bare life that more and more can no longer be inscribed in that order. The growing dissociation of birth (bare life) and the nation-state is the new fact of politics in our day, and what we call *camp* is this disjunction. To an order without localization (the state of exception, in which law is suspended) there now corresponds a localization without order (the camp as permanent space of exception). The political system no longer orders forms of life and juridical rules in a determinate space, but instead contains at its very center a *dislocating localization* that exceeds it and into which every form of life and every rule can be virtually taken. The camp as dislocating localization is the hidden matrix of the politics in which we are still living, and it is this structure of the camp that we must learn to recognize in all its metamorphoses into the *zones d'attentes* of our airports and certain outskirts of our cities. The camp is the fourth, inseparable element that has now added itself to—and so broken—the old trinity composed of the state, the nation (birth), and land.

From this perspective, the camps have, in a certain sense, reappeared in an even more extreme form in the territories of the former Yugoslavia. What is happening there is by no means, as interested observers have been quick to declare, a redefinition of the old political system according to new ethnic and territorial arrangements, which is to say, a simple repetition of processes that led to the constitution of the European nation-states. At issue in the former Yugoslavia is, rather, an incurable rupture of the old *nomos* and a dislocation of populations and human lives along entirely new lines of flight. Hence the decisive importance of ethnic rape camps. If the Nazis never thought of effecting the Final Solution by making Jewish women pregnant, it is because the principle of birth that assured the inscription of life in the order of the nation-state was still—if in a profoundly transformed sense— in operation. This principle has now entered into a process of decay and dislocation. It is becoming increasingly impossible for it to function, and we must expect not only new camps but also always new and more lunatic regulative definitions of the inscription of life in the city. The camp, which is now securely lodged within the city's interior, is the new biopolitical *nomos* of the planet.

א Every interpretation of the political meaning of the term "people" must begin with the singular fact that in modern European languages, "people" also always indicates the poor, the disinherited, and the excluded. One term thus names both the constitutive political subject and the class that is, de facto if not de jure, excluded from politics.

In common speech as in political parlance, the Italian *popolo*, the French *peuple*, the Spanish *pueblo* (like the corresponding adjectives *popolare*, *populaire*, *popolar* and late Latin *populus* and *popularis*, from which they derive) designate both the complex of citizens as a unitary political body (as in "the Italian people" or "the people's judge") and the members of the lower classes (as in *homme du peuple*, *rione popolare*, *front populaire*). Even the English word "people," which has a less differentiated meaning, still conserves the sense of "ordinary people" in contrast to the rich and the nobility. In the American Constitution one thus reads, without any distinction, "We the people of the United States." Yet when Lincoln invokes a "Government of the people, by the people, for the people" in the Gettysburg Address, the repetition implicitly opposes the first "people" to another "people." Just how essential this ambiguity was even during the French Revolution (that is, at precisely the point at which claims were made for the principle of popular sovereignty) is shown by the decisive role played by compassion for the people under-stood as an excluded class. Arendt noted that "the very definition of the word was born out of compassion, and the term became the equivalent for misfortune and unhappiness—*le peuple, les malheureux m'applaudis-sent,* as Robespierre was wont to say; *le peuple toujours malheureux,* as even Sieyès, one of the least sentimental and most sober figures of the Revolution, would put it" (*On Revolution,* p. 70). But in the chapter of Bodin's *Republic* in which democracy or the *état populaire* is defined, the concept is already double: as the titular holder of sovereignty, the *peuple en corps* is contrasted with the *menu peuple,* whom wisdom counsels excluding from political power.

Such a diffuse and constant semantic ambiguity cannot be accidental: it must reflect an amphiboly inherent in the nature and function of the concept "people" in Western politics. It is as if what we call "people" were in reality not a unitary subject but a dialectical oscillation between two opposite poles: on the one hand, the set of the People as a whole political body, and on the other, the subset of the people as a fragmentary multiplicity of needy and excluded bodies; or again, on the one hand, an inclusion that claims to be total, and on the other, an exclusion that is clearly hopeless; at one extreme, the total state of integrated and sovereign citizens, and at the other, the preserve—court of miracles or camp—of the wretched, the oppressed, and the defeated. In this sense, a single and compact referent for the term "people" simply does not exist anywhere: like many fundamental political concepts (similar, in this respect, to the *Urworte* of Abel and Freud or to L. Dumont's hierarchical relations), "people" is a polar concept that indicates a double movement and a complex relation between two extremes. But this also means that the constitution of the human species in a political body passes through a fundamental division and that in the concept "people" we can easily recognize the categorial pairs that we have seen to define the original political structure: bare life (people) and political existence (People), exclusion and inclusion, *zoē* and *bios.* The "people" thus always already carries the

fundamental biopolitical fracture within itself. It is what cannot be included in the whole of which it is a part and what cannot belong to the
set in which it is always already included. Hence the contradictions and
aporias to which it gives rise every time that it is evoked and put into play
on the political scene. It is what always already *is* and yet must, nevertheless, be realized; it is the pure source of every identity but must, however, continually be redefined and purified through exclusion, language,
blood, and land. Or, at the opposite pole, the "people" is what is by
essence lacking to itself and that whose realization therefore coincides
with its own abolition; it is what must, together with its opposite, negate
itself in order to be (hence the specific aporias of the workers' movement,
turned toward the people and, at the same time, toward its abolition). At
times the bloody flag of reaction and the uncertain insignia of revolutions
and popular fronts, the people always contains a division more originary
than that of friend-enemy, an incessant civil war that divides it more
radically than every conflict and, at the same time, keeps it united and
constitutes it more securely than any identity. When one looks closely,
even what Marx called "class conflict," which occupies such a central
place in his thought—though it remains substantially undefined—is
nothing other than the civil war that divides every people and that will
come to an end only when, in the classless society or the messianic
kingdom, People and people will coincide and there will no longer be,
strictly speaking, any people.

   If this is true, if the people necessarily contains the fundamental
biopolitical fracture within itself, then it will be possible to read certain
decisive pages of the history of our century in a new way. For if the
struggle between the two "peoples" was certainly always under way, in
our time it has experienced a final, paroxysmal acceleration. In Rome, the
internal division of the people was juridically sanctioned by the clear
division between *populus* and *plebs*, each of which had its own institutions and magistrates, just as in the Middle Ages the distinction between
the *popolo minuto* and the *popolo grasso*[2] corresponded to a precise
ordering of various arts and trades. But starting with the French Revolution, when it becomes the sole depositary of sovereignty, the people is
transformed into an embarrassing presence, and misery and exclusion

   2. In thirteenth-century Florence, *popolo minuto* referred to the class of
artisans and tradespeople and *popolo grasso* referred to the commercial classes and
bourgeoisie.—Trans.

appear for the first time as an altogether intolerable scandal. In the modern era, misery and exclusion are not only economic or social concepts but eminently political categories (all the economism and "socialism" that seem to dominate modern politics actually have a political—and even a biopolitical—significance).

In this sense, our age is nothing but the implacable and methodical attempt to overcome the division dividing the people, to eliminate radically the people that is excluded. This attempt brings together, according to different modalities and horizons, Right and Left, capitalist countries and socialist countries, which are united in the project—which is in the last analysis futile but which has been partially realized in all industrialized countries—of producing a single and undivided people. The obsession with development is as effective as it is in our time because it coincides with the biopolitical project to produce an undivided people.

The extermination of the Jews in Nazi Germany acquires a radically new significance in this light. As the people that refuses to be integrated into the national political body (it is assumed that every assimilation is actually only simulated), the Jews are the representatives par excellence and almost the living symbol of the people and of the bare life that modernity necessarily creates within itself, but whose presence it can no longer tolerate in any way. And we must see the extreme phase of the internal struggle that divides People and people in the lucid fury with which the German *Volk*—representative par excellence of the People as a whole political body—sought to eliminate the Jews forever. With the Final Solution (which did, not by chance, involve Gypsies and others who could not be integrated), Nazism darkly and futilely sought to liberate the political scene of the West from this intolerable shadow in order to produce the German *Volk* as the people that finally overcame the original biopolitical fracture. (This is why the Nazi leaders so obstinately repeated that in eliminating Jews and Gypsies, they were actually also working for the other European peoples.)

Paraphrasing the Freudian postulate on the relation between ego and id, one could say that modern biopolitics is supported by the principle according to which "Where there is bare life, there will have to be a People"—on condition that one immediately add that the principle also holds in its inverse formulation: "Where there is a People, there will be bare life." The fracture that was believed to have been overcome by eliminating the people (the Jews who are its symbol) thus reproduces itself anew, transforming the entire German people into a sacred life consecrated to death, and a biological body that must be infinitely purified (through the elimination of the mentally ill and the bearers of hereditary diseases). And in a different yet analogous way, today's democratico-capitalist project of eliminating the poor classes through development not only reproduces within itself the people that is excluded but also transforms the entire population of the Third World into bare life. Only a politics that will have learned to take the fundamental biopolitical fracture of the West into account will be able to stop this oscillation and to put an end to the civil war that divides the peoples and the cities of the earth.

§ Threshold

Three theses have emerged as provisional conclusions in the course of this inquiry:

1. The original political relation is the ban (the state of exception as zone of indistinction between outside and inside, exclusion and inclusion).

2. The fundamental activity of sovereign power is the production of bare life as originary political element and as threshold of articulation between nature and culture, *zoē* and *bios*.

3. Today it is not the city but rather the camp that is the fundamental biopolitical paradigm of the West.

The first of these theses calls into question every theory of the contractual origin of state power and, along with it, every attempt to ground political communities in something like a "belonging," whether it be founded on popular, national, religious, or any other identity. The second thesis implies that Western politics is a biopolitics from the very beginning, and that every attempt to found political liberties in the rights of the citizen is, therefore, in vain. The third thesis, finally, throws a sinister light on the models by which social sciences, sociology, urban studies, and architecture today are trying to conceive and organize the public space of the world's cities without any clear awareness that at their very center lies the same bare life (even if it has been transformed and rendered apparently more human) that defined the biopolitics of the great totalitarian states of the twentieth century.

In the syntagm "bare life," "bare" corresponds to the Greek *haplōs*, the term by which first philosophy defines pure Being. The isolation of the sphere of pure Being, which constitutes the fundamental activity of Western metaphysics, is not without analogies with the isolation of bare life in the realm of Western politics. What constitutes man as a thinking animal has its exact counterpart in what constitutes him as a political animal. In the first case, the problem is to isolate pure Being (*on haplōs*) from the many meanings of the term "Being" (which, according to Aristotle, "is said in many ways"); in the second, what is at stake is the separation of bare life from the many forms of concrete life. Pure Being, bare life—what is contained in these two concepts, such that both the metaphysics and the politics of the West find their foundation and sense in them and in them alone? What is the link between the two constitutive processes by which metaphysics and politics seem, in isolating their proper element, simultaneously to run up against an unthinkable limit? For bare life is certainly as indeterminate and impenetrable as *haplōs* Being, and one could say that reason cannot think bare life except as it thinks pure Being, in stupor and in astonishment (*almost astonished*, Schelling).

Yet precisely these two empty and indeterminate concepts seem to safeguard the keys to the historico-political destiny of the West. And it may be that only if we are able to decipher the political meaning of pure Being will we be able to master the bare life that expresses our subjection to political power, just as it may be, inversely, that only if we understand the theoretical implications of bare life will we be able to solve the enigma of ontology. Brought to the limit of pure Being, metaphysics (thought) passes over into politics (into reality), just as on the threshold of bare life, politics steps beyond itself into theory.

Georges Dumézil and Károly Kerényi have described the life of the *Flamen Diale*, one of the greatest priests of classical Rome. His life is remarkable in that it is at every moment indistinguishable from the cultic functions that the *Flamen* fulfills. This is why the Romans said that the *Flamen Diale* is *quotidie feriatus* and *assiduus sacerdos*, that is, in an act of uninterrupted celebration at every instant. Accordingly, there is no gesture or detail of his life, the way he dresses or the way he walks, that does not have a precise meaning and is not caught in a series of functions and meticulously studied effects. As proof of this "assiduity," the *Flamen* is not allowed to take his emblems off completely even in sleep; the hair and nails that are cut from his body must be immediately buried under an *arbor felix* (that is, a tree that is not sacred to the gods of the underworld); in his clothes there can be neither knots not closed rings, and he cannot swear oaths; if he meets a prisoner in fetters while on a stroll, the prisoner's bonds must be undone; he cannot enter into a bower in which vine shoots are hanging; he must abstain from raw meat and every kind of leavened flour and successfully avoid fava beans, dogs, she-goats, and ivy ...

In the life of the *Flamen Diale* it is not possible to isolate something like a bare life. All of the *Flamen's* *zoē* has become *bios*; private sphere and public function are now absolutely identical. This is why Plutarch (with a formula that recalls the Greek and medieval definition of the sovereign as *lex animata*) can say that he is *hōsper empsuchon kai hieron agalma*, a sacred living statue.

Let us now observe the life of *homo sacer*, or of the bandit, the *Friedlos*, the *aquae et igni interdictus*, which are in many ways similar. He has been excluded from the religious community and from all political life: he cannot participate in the rites of his *gens*, nor (if he has been declared *infamis et intestabilis*) can he perform any juridically valid act. What is more, his entire existence is reduced to a bare life stripped of every right by virtue of the fact that anyone can kill him without committing homicide; he can save himself only in perpetual flight or a foreign land. And yet he is in a continuous relationship with the power that banished him precisely insofar as he is at every instant exposed to an unconditioned threat of death. He is pure *zoē*, but his *zoē* is as such caught in the sovereign ban and must reckon with it at every moment, finding the best way to elude or deceive it. In this sense, no life, as exiles and bandits know well, is more "political" than his.

Now consider the person of the Führer in the Third Reich. He represents the unity and equality of stock of the German people (Schmitt, "Staat," p. 42). His is not a despot's or a dictator's authority, which is imposed on the will and the persons of the subjects from outside (ibid., pp. 41–42). His power is, rather, all the more unlimited insofar as he is identified with the very biological life of the German people. By virtue of this identity, his every word is immediately law (*Führerworte haben Gesetzkraft*, as Eichmann did not tire of repeating at his trial in Jerusalem), and he recognizes himself immediately in his own command (*zu seinem Befehl sich bekennenden* [Schmitt, "Führertum," p. 679]). He can certainly have a private life, but what defines him as Führer is that his existence as such has an immediately political character. Thus while the office of the chancellor of the Reich is a public *dignitas* received on the basis of procedures foreseen in the Weimar constitution, the office of the Führer is no longer an office in the sense of traditional public law, but rather something that springs forth without mediation from his person insofar as it coincides with the life of the German people. The Führer is the political form of this life: this is why his word is law and why he demands nothing of the German people except what it in truth already is.

Here the traditional distinction between the sovereign's political body and his physical body (whose genealogy Kantorowicz has patiently reconstructed) disappears, and the two bodies are drastically contracted into one. The Führer has, so to speak, a whole body that is neither private nor public and whose life is in itself supremely political. The Führer's body is, in other words, situated at the point of coincidence between *zoē* and *bios*, biological body and political body. In his person, *zoē* and *bios* incessantly pass over into each other.

Now imagine the most extreme figure of the camp inhabitant. Primo Levi has described the person who in camp jargon was called "the Muslim," *der Muselmann*—a being from whom humiliation, horror, and fear had so taken away all consciousness and all personality as to make him absolutely apathetic (hence the ironical name given to him). He was not only, like his companions, excluded from the political and social context to which he once belonged; he was not only, as Jewish life that does not deserve to live, destined to a future more or less close to death. He no longer belongs to the world of men in any way; he does not even belong to the threatened and precarious world of the camp inhabitants who have forgotten him from the very beginning. Mute and absolutely alone, he has passed into another world without memory and without grief. For him, Hölderlin's statement that "at the extreme limit of pain, nothing remains but the conditions of time and space" holds to the letter.

What is the life of the *Muselmann*? Can one say that it is pure *zoē*? Nothing "natural" or "common," however, is left in him; nothing animal or instinctual remains in his life. All his instincts are canceled along with his reason. Antelme tells us that the camp inhabitant was no longer capable of distinguishing between pangs of cold and the ferocity of the SS. If we apply this statement to the *Muselmann* quite literally ("the cold, SS"), then we can say that he moves in an absolute indistinction of fact and law, of life and juridical rule, and of nature and politics. Because of this, the guard suddenly seems powerless before him, as if struck by the thought that the *Muselmann*'s behavior—which does not register any difference between an order and the cold—might perhaps be a silent form of resistance. Here a law that seeks to transform itself entirely into life finds itself confronted with a life that is absolutely indistinguishable from law, and it is precisely this indiscernibility that threatens the *lex animata* of the camp.

Paul Rabinow refers to the case of Wilson, the biochemist who decided to make his own body and life into a research and experimentation laboratory upon discovering that he suffered from leukemia. Since he is accountable only to himself, the barriers between ethics and law disappear; scientific research can freely and fully coincide with biography. His body is no longer private, since it has been transformed into a laboratory; but neither is it public, since only insofar as it is his own body can he transgress the limits that morality and law put to experimentation. "Experimental life" is the term Rabinow uses to define Wilson's life. It is easy to see that "experimental life" is a *bios* that has, in a very particular sense, so concentrated itself on its own *zoē* as to become indistinguishable from it.

We enter the hospital room where the body of Karen Quinlan or the overcomatose person is lying, or where the neomort is waiting for his organs to be transplanted. Here biological life—which the machines are keeping functional by artificial respiration, pumping blood into the arteries, and regulating the blood temperature—has been entirely separated from the form of life that bore the name Karen Quinlan: here life becomes (or at least seems to become) pure *zoē*. When physiology made its appearance in the history of medical science toward the middle of the seventeenth century, it was defined in relation to anatomy, which had dominated the birth and the development of modern medicine. And if anatomy (which was grounded in the dissection of the dead body) was the description of inert organs, physiology is "an anatomy in motion," the explanation of the function of organs in the living body. Karen Quinlan's body is really only anatomy in motion, a set of functions whose purpose is no longer the life of an organism. Her life is maintained only by means of life-support technology and by virtue of a legal decision. It is no longer life, but rather death in motion. And yet since life and death are now merely biopolitical concepts, as we have seen, Karen Quinlan's body—which wavers between life and death according to the progress of medicine and the changes in legal decisions—is a legal being as much as it is a biological being. A law that seeks to decide on life is embodied in a life that coincides with death.

The choice of this brief series of "lives" may seem extreme, if not arbitrary. Yet the list could well have continued with cases no less extreme and still more familiar: the Bosnian woman at Omarska, a perfect threshold of indistinction between biology and politics, or—in an apparently opposite, yet analogous, sense—military interventions on humanitarian grounds, in which war efforts are carried out for the sake of biological ends such as nutrition or the care of epidemics (which is just as clear an example of an undecidability between politics and biology).

It is on the basis of these uncertain and nameless terrains, these difficult zones of indistinction, that the ways and the forms of a new politics must be thought. At the end of the first volume of the *History of Sexuality*, having distanced himself from the sex and sexuality in which modernity, caught in nothing other than a deployment of power, believed it would find its own secret and liberation, Foucault alludes to a "different economy of bodies and pleasures" as a possible horizon for a different politics. The conclusions of our study force us to be more cautious. Like the concepts of sex and sexuality, the concept of the "body" too is always already caught in a deployment of power. The "body" is always already a biopolitical body and bare life, and nothing in it or the economy of its pleasure seems to allow us to find solid ground on which to oppose the demands of sovereign power. In its extreme form, the biopolitical body of the West (this last incarnation of *homo sacer*) appears as a threshold of absolute indistinction between law and fact, juridical rule and biological life. In the person of the Führer, bare life passes immediately into law, just as in the person of the camp inhabitant (or the neomort) law becomes indistinguishable from biological life. Today a law that seeks to transform itself wholly into life is more and more confronted with a life that has been deadened and mortified into juridical rule. Every attempt to rethink the political space of the West must begin with the clear awareness that we no longer know anything of the classical distinction between *zoē* and *bios*, between private life and political existence, between man as a simple living being at home in the house and man's political existence in the city. This is why the restoration of classical political categories proposed by Leo Strauss and, in a different sense, by Hannah Arendt can have only a critical sense.

There is no return from the camps to classical politics. In the camps, city and house became indistinguishable, and the possibility of differentiating between our biological body and our political body—between what is incommunicable and mute and what is communicable and sayable—was taken from us forever. And we are not only, in Foucault's words, animals whose life as living beings is at issue in their politics, but also—inversely—citizens whose very politics is at issue in their natural body.

Just as the biopolitical body of the West cannot be simply given back to its natural life in the *oikos*, so it cannot be overcome in a passage to a new body—a technical body or a wholly political or glorious body—in which a different economy of pleasures and vital functions would once and for all resolve the interlacement of *zoē* and *bios* that seems to define the political destiny of the West. This biopolitical body that is bare life must itself instead be transformed into the site for the constitution and installation of a form of life that is wholly exhausted in bare life and a *bios* that is only its own *zoē*. Here attention will also have to be given to the analogies between politics and the epochal situation of metaphysics. Today *bios* lies in *zoē* exactly as essence, in the Heideggerian definition of Dasein, lies (*liegt*) in existence. Yet how can a *bios* be only its own *zoē*, how can a form of life seize hold of the very *haplōs* that constitutes both the task and the enigma of Western metaphysics? If we give the name form-of-life to this being that is only its own bare existence and to this life that, being its own form, remains inseparable from it, we will witness the emergence of a field of research beyond the terrain defined by the intersection of politics and philosophy, medico-biological sciences and jurisprudence. First, however, it will be necessary to examine how it was possible for something like a bare life to be conceived within these disciplines, and how the historical development of these very disciplines has brought them to a limit beyond which they cannot venture without risking an unprecedented biopolitical catastrophe.

Bibliography

Translator's note: The bibliography contains only those works cited in the text. In the case of works not originally published in English, the translations listed below were consulted; but all passages quoted in the text have been newly translated. Page references refer to works as they are first listed here.

Abel, K. *Sprachwissenschaftliche Abhandlungen.* Leipzig: W. Friedrich, 1885. (*Linguistic Essays.* London: Trubner, 1882.)

Antelme, Robert. *L'espèce humaine.* Paris: Gallimard, 1994. (*The Human Race.* Trans. Jeffrey Haight and Annie Mahler. Malboro, Vt.: Malboro Press, 1992.)

Arendt, Hannah. *Essays in Understanding, 1930–1954.* Ed. Jerome Kohn. New York: Harcourt & Brace, 1994.

———. *On Revolution.* New York: Viking, 1963.

———. *The Origins of Totalitarianism.* New York: Harcourt Brace Jovanovich, 1979.

Badiou, Alain. *L'être et l'événement.* Paris: Seuil, 1988.

Bataille, Georges. "Hegel, la mort et le sacrifice." In Georges Bataille, *Oeuvres complètes*, vol. 12. Paris: Gallimard, 1988. ("Hegel, Death, and Sacrifice." *Yale French Studies*, 78 [1990].)

———. *La souveraineté.* In Georges Bataille, *Oeuvres complètes*, vol. 8. Paris: Gallimard, 1976.

Benjamin, Walter. *Briefe.* Ed. Gerschom Scholem and Theodor W. Adorno. Vol. 1. Frankfurt am Main: Suhrkamp, 1966. (*The Correspon-*

dence of Walter Benjamin, 1919–1940. Ed. Gerschom Scholem and Theodor W. Adorno. Trans. Manfred R. Jacobsen and Evelyn M. Jacobsen. Chicago: University of Chicago Press, 1994.)

———. *Gesammelte Schriften.* Ed. Rolf Tiedemann and Hermann Schweppenhäuser. 2 vols. Frankfurt am Main: Suhrkamp, 1974–89.

———. "Über den Begriff der Geschichte." In Benjamin, *Gesammelte Schriften,* vol. 1, 2. ("Theses on the Philosophy of History." Trans. Harry Zohn. In Walter Benjamin, *Illuminations,* ed. Hannah Arendt. New York: Schocken Books, 1968.)

———. *Ursprung des deutschen Trauerspiels.* In Benjamin, *Gesammelte Schriften,* vol. 1, 1. (*The Origin of the German Tragic Drama.* Trans. John Osborne. London: Verso, 1985.)

———. "Zur Kritik der Gewalt." In Benjamin, *Gesammelte Schriften,* vol. 2, 1. ("Critique of Violence." Trans. Edmund Jephcott. In Walter Benjamin, *Reflections,* ed. Peter Demetz. New York: Schocken Books, 1978.)

Benjamin, Walter, and Gerschom Scholem. *Briefwechsel 1933–1940.* Ed. Gerschom Scholem. Frankfurt am Main: Suhrkamp, 1988. (*The Correspondence of Walter Benjamin and Gerschom Scholem, 1932–1940.* Ed. Gerschom Scholem. Trans. Gary Smith and Andre Lefevere. Cambridge, Mass.: Harvard University Press, 1992.)

Bennett, H. "Sacer esto." *Transactions of the American Philological Association,* 61 (1930).

Benveniste, Émile. *Le vocabulaire des institutions indo-européennes.* Vol. 2. Paris: Minuit, 1969. (*Indo-European Language and Society.* Trans. Elizabeth Palmer. Coral Gables: University of Florida Press, 1973.)

Bickermann, Elias. *Consecratio, Le culte des souverains dans l'empire romain.* Entretiens Hardt, XIX. Geneva: 1972.

———. "Die römische Kaiserapotheose." *Archiv für Religionswissenschaft,* 27 (1929).

Binding, Karl, and Alfred Hoche. *Die Freigabe der Vernichtung lebensunwerten Lebens.* Leipzig: F. Meiner, 1920. (*The Release of the Destruction of Life Devoid of Value: Its Measure and Its Form.* Santa Ana, Calif.: R. L. Sassone, 1975.)

Blanchot, Maurice. *L'entretien infini.* Paris: Gallimard, 1969. (*The Infinite Conversation.* Trans. Susan Hanson. Minneapolis: University of Minnesota Press, 1993.)

Bodin, Jean. *Les six livres de la République.* Paris: n.p., 1583. (*The Six Books of the Commonweale.* Ed. Kenneth D. McKae. New York: Arno, 1979.)

Burdeau, G. *Traité de science politique.* Vol. 4. Paris: Librarie génerale du droit et de jurisprudence, 1984.

Cacciari, Massimo. *Icone della legge.* Milan: Adelphi, 1985.

Callois, Roger. *L'homme et le sacré.* Paris: Presses Universitaires de France, 1939. (*Man and the Sacred.* Trans. Meyer Barash. Westport, Conn.: Greenwood, 1980.)

Cavalca, Desiderio. *Il bando nella prassi e nella dottrina medievale.* Milan: A. Giuffra, 1978.

Crifò, Giuliano. *L'esclusione dalla città: Altri studi sull'exilium romano.* Perugia: Università di Perugia, 1985.

——. "Exilica causa, quae adversus exulem agitur." In *Du châtiment dans la cité: Supplices corporels et peine de mort dans le monde antique.* Rome: L'École française de Rome, 1984.

Dagognet, François. *La maîtrise du vivant.* Paris: Hachette, 1988.

Deleuze, Gilles, and Félix Guattari. *Mille plateaux.* Paris: Minuit, 1980. (*A Thousand Plateaus: Capitalism and Schizophrenia.* Trans. Brian Massumi. Minneapolis: University of Minnesota Press, 1987.)

De Romilly, Jacqueline. *La loi dans la pensée greque des origines à Aristote.* Paris: Les belles Lettres, 1971.

Derrida, Jacques. "Force of Law." *Cardozo Law Review,* 11 (1990).

——. "Préjugés." In *Spiegel und Gleichnis,* ed. N. W. Bolz and W. Hübener. Würzburg: Königshausen und Neumann, 1983. ("Before the Law." Trans. Avital Ronnell and Christine Roulston. In Jacques Derrida, *Acts of Literature,* ed. Derek Attridge. London: Routledge, 1992.)

Drobisch, Klaus, and Günter Wieland. *System der NS-Konzentrationslager 1933–39.* Berlin: Akademie Verlag, 1993.

Durkheim, Émile. *Les formes élémentaires de la vie réligieuse.* Paris: F. Alcan, 1912. (*The Elementary Forms of Religious Life.* Trans. Karen E. Fields. New York: Free Press, 1995.)

Ehrenberg, Victor. *Rechtsidee im frühen Griechentum.* Leipzig: S. Hirzel, 1921.

Foucault, Michel. *Dits et écrits.* Vols. 3–4. Paris: Gallimard, 1994.

——. *La volonté de savoir.* Paris: Gallimard, 1976. (*History of Sexuality, Volume I: An Introduction.* Trans. Robert Hurley. New York: Random House, 1978.)

Fowler, W. Ward. *Roman Essays and Interpretation.* Oxford: Clarendon Press, 1920.

Freud, Sigmund. "Über den Gegensinn der Urworte." *Jahrbuch für psychoanalytische und psychopathologische Forschungen,* 11 (1910). ("The

Antithetical Meaning of Primal Words." Trans. Alan Tyson. In *The Standard Edition of the Complete Psychological Works of Sigmund Freud*, ed. James Strachey, vol. 11. London: Hogarth Press, 1957.)

Fugier, Huguette. *Recherches sur l'expression du sacré dans la langue latine*. Paris: Les belles Lettres, 1963.

Furet, François, ed. *L'Allemagne nazi et le génocide juif.* Paris: Seuil, 1985. (*Unanswered Questions: Nazi Germany and the Genocide of the Jews*. New York: Schocken, 1989.)

Gaylin, W. "Harvesting the Dead." *Harper's*, September 23, 1974.

Giesey, Ralph E. *Cérémonial et puissance souveraine*. Paris: A. Colin, 1987.

——. *The Royal Funeral Ceremony in Renaissance France*. Geneva: E. Droz, 1960.

Harvard University Medical School. "A Definition of Irreversible Coma." *JAMA*, 205 (1968). Cited in text as the Harvard Report.

Hegel, Georg Wilhelm Friedrich. *Phänomenologie des Geistes*. In G. W. F. Hegel, *Werke in zwanzig Bänden*, vol. 3. Frankfurt: Suhrkamp, 1971. (*Phenomenology of Spirit*. Trans. A. V. Miller. Oxford: Oxford University Press, 1977.)

Heidegger, Martin. *Beiträge zur Philosophie*. In Martin Heidegger, *Gesamtausgabe*, vol. 65. Frankfurt am Main: Vittorio Klostermann, 1989.

——. *Einführung in die Metaphysik*. Tübingen: Max Niemeyer, 1962. (*An Introduction to Metaphysics*. Trans. Ralph Manheim. New Haven, Conn.: Yale University Press, 1959.)

——. *Zur Sache des Denkens*. Tübingen: Max Niemeyer, 1976. (*On Time and Being*. Trans. Joan Stambaugh. New York: Harper and Row, 1972.)

Hobbes, Thomas. *De cive: The Latin Version*. Ed. Howard Warrender. Oxford: Clarendon Press, 1983.

——. *De homine*. In Thomas Hobbes, *Opera philosophica quae latine scripsit omnia in unum corpus*, ed. William Molesworth, vol. 2. London: Apud J. Bohn, 1983.

——. *Leviathan*. Ed. R. Tuck. Cambridge: Cambridge University Press, 1991.

Hölderlin, Friedrich. *Sämtliche Werke*. Ed. Friedrich Beißner. Vol. 5. Stuttgart: J. G. Cottasche Buchhandlung Nachfolger, 1954.

Jhering, Rodolphe. *L'esprit du droit romain dans les diverses phases de son développement*. Trans. O. de Meulenaere. Vol. 1. Paris: Marescq, 1886.

Kant, Immanuel. *Kants opus postuum*. Ed. Adickes. Berlin: Reuther & Reichard, 1920. (*Opus Postuum. Cambridge Edition of the Works of*

Immanuel Kant. Trans. Eckhard Förster. Cambridge, Eng.: Cambridge University Press, 1993).

——. *Kritik der praktischen Vernunft.* In *Kants Gesammelte Schriften,* Akademieausgabe, vol. 5. Berlin: G. Reimer, 1913. (*Critique of Practical Reason.* Trans. Lewis White Beck. New York: Macmillan, 1993.)

——. "Über den Gemeinspruch: Das mag in der Theorie richtig sein, taugt aber nicht für die Praxis." In *Kants Gesammelte Schriften,* Akademieausgabe, vol. 8. Berlin: G. Reimer, 1914. ("On the Common Saying: 'This May Be True in Theory, but It Does Not Apply in Practice." In *Kant, Political Writings,* ed. Hans Riess, trans. N. B. Nisbet. Cambridge, Eng.: Cambridge University Press, 1991).

Kantorowicz, Ernst Hartwig. *The King's Two Bodies: A Study in Mediaeval Political Theology.* Princeton, N.J.: Princeton University Press, 1957.

Kerényi, Károly. *La religione antica nelle sue linee fondamentali.* Trans. Delio Cantimori. Bologna: N. Zanichelli, 1940.

Kojève, Alexandre. "Les romans de la sagesse." *Critique,* 60 (1952).

La Cecla, Franco. *Mente locale: Per un'antropologia dell'abitare.* Milan: Eleuthra, 1993.

Lamb, David. *Death, Brain Death, and Ethics.* Albany: State University of New York Press, 1985.

Lange, Ludwig. "De consecratione capitis." In Ludwig Lange, *Kleine Schriften aus dem Gebiete der Classischen,* vol. 2 Göttingen: Vandenhoek & Ruprecht, 1887.

Lefort, Claude. *Écrire à l'épreuve du politique.* Paris: Calmann-Levy, 1992.

Levi, Carlo. *Cristo si è fermato a Eboli.* Turin: Einaudi, 1946. (*Christ Stopped at Eboli: The Story of a Year.* Trans. Frances Frenaye. New York: Terpio, 1982.)

Levinas, Emmanuel. "Quelques réflexions sur la philosophie de l'Hitlerisme." *Esprit,* 26 (1934).

——. "Reflections on the Philosophy of Hitlerism." Trans. Séan Hand. *Critical Inquiry,* 17 (1990).

Lévi-Strauss, Claude. "Introduction à l'œuvre de Marcel Mauss." In Marcel Mauss, *Sociologie et anthropologie.* Paris: Presses Universitaire de France, 1950.

Livy. *Ab urbe condita libri.* Vol. 4. Trans. B. O. Forster. Loeb Classical Library. Cambridge, Mass.: Harvard University Press, 1948.

Löwith, Karl. *Der okkasionelle Dezionismus von Carl Schmitt.* In Karl Löwith, *Sämtliche Schriften,* ed. Klaus Stichweh and Marc B. de Launay, vol. 8. Stuttgart: Metzler, 1984.

Magdelain, André. *La loi de Rome. Histoire d'un concept.* Paris: Les belles Lettres, 1978.

Mairet, Gérard. *Histoire des idéologies, sous la direction de François Châtelet and Gérard Mairet.* Vol. 3. Paris: Hachette, 1978.

Mauss, Marcel, and H. Hubert. "Essai sur la nature et la fonction du sacrifice." In Marcel Mauss, *Œuvres,* vol. 1. Paris: Gallimard, 1968.

Milner, J.-C. "L'exemple et la fiction." In *Transparence et opacité: Littérature et sciences cognitives,* ed. Tibor Papp and Pierre Pira. Paris: Cerf, 1988.

Mitscherlich, Alexander, and F. Mielke. *Wissenschaft ohne Menschlichkeit. Medizinische und Eugenische Irrwege unter Diktatur, Burokratie und Krieg.* Heidelberg: Schneider, 1949. (*The Death Doctors.* Trans. James Cleugh. London: Elek Books, 1962.)

Mollaret, P., and M. Goulon. "Le coma dépassé." *Revue neurologique,* 101 (1959).

Mommsen, Theodor. *Römisches Strafrecht.* Leipzig: Duncker & Humbolt, 1889.

Muratori, Lodovico Antonio. *Antiquitates italicae Medii Aevi.* Vol. 2. Milan: Mediolani, 1739.

Nancy, Jean-Luc. *L'impératif catégorique.* Paris: Flammarion, 1983. ("Abandoned Being." In Jean-Luc Nancy, *The Birth to Presence,* trans. Brian Holmes. Stanford, Calif.: Stanford University Press, 1993.)

Negri, Antonio. *Il potere costituente: Saggio sulle alternative del moderno.* Milan: SugarCo, 1992.

Otto, Rudolph. *Das Heilige: Über das Irrationelle in der Idee des Göttlichen und sein Verhältnis zum Rationalen.* Breslau: Trewendt und Granier, 1917. (*The Idea of the Holy: An Inquiry into the Non-Rational Factor in the Idea of the Divine and Its Relation to the Rational.* Trans. John W. Harvey. Oxford: Oxford University Press, 1970.)

Rosenberg, Alfred. *Blut und Ehre, Ein Kampf für deutsche Wiedergeburt. Reden und Aufsätze 1919–1933.* Munich: F. Eher nachf., 1936.

Schilling, Robert. "Sacrum et profanum, Essais d'interprétation." *Latomus,* 30 (1971).

Schmitt, Carl. "Führertum als Grundbegriff des nationalsozialistischen Rechts." *Europäische Revue,* 9 (1933).

———. *Das Nomos von der Erde.* Berlin: Duncker & Humbolt, 1974.

———. *Politische Theologie, Vier Kapitel zur Lehre von der Souveränität.* Munich-Leipzig: Duncker & Humbolt, 1922. (*Political Theology: Four*

Chapters on the Concept of Sovereignty. Trans. George Schwab. Cambridge, Mass.: MIT Press, 1985.)

———. "Staat, Bewegung, Volk." In Carl Schmitt, *Die Dreigliederung der politischen Einheit.* Hamburg: Hanseatische Verlagsanstalt, 1933.

———. *Theorie des Partisanen, Zwischenbemerkung zum Begriff des Politischen.* Berlin: Duncker & Humbolt, 1963.

———. *Über Schuld und Schuldarten, Eine terminologische Untersuchung.* Breslau: Schletter, 1910.

———. *Verfassungslehre.* Munich-Leipzig: Duncker & Humbolt, 1928.

Sewell, W. H. "Le citoyen/La citoyenne: Activity, Passivity, and the Revolutionary Concept of Citizenship." In *The French Revolution and the Creation of Modern Political Culture,* ed. Lucas Colin. Oxford: Pergamon, 1988.

Sieyès, Emmanuel-Joseph. *Écrits politiques.* Paris: Éditions des Archives contemporains, 1985.

———. *Qu'est ce que le Tiers État?* Paris: 1789. (*What Is the Third Estate?* Trans. M. Blondel. London: Pall Mall, 1963.)

Smith, William Robertson. *Lectures on the Religion of the Semites.* London: A & C Black, 1894.

Stier, H. E. "Nomos basileus." *Philologus,* 82 (1928).

Strachan-Davidson, James Leigh. *Problems of Roman Criminal Law.* Vol. 1. Oxford: Clarendon, 1912.

Svenbro, Jesper. *Phrasikleia, Anthropologie de la lecture en Grèce ancienne.* Paris: La Découverte, 1988. (*Phrasikleia: An Anthropology of Reading in Ancient Greece.* Trans. Janet Lloyd. Ithaca, N.Y.: Cornell University Press, 1993.)

Thomas, Yan. "Vita necisque potestas: Le père, la cité, la mort." In *Du châtiment das la cité: Supplices corporels et peine de mort dans le monde antique.* Rome: L'École française de Rome, 1984.

Vernant, Jean-Pierre. *Mythe et pensée chez les Grecs.* Paris: François Maspero, 1965. (*Myth and Thought Among the Greeks.* London: Routledge and Kegan Paul, 1983.)

Verschuer, Otmar Freiherr von. *Rassenhygiene als Wissenschaft und Staatsaufgabe.* Frankfurt, 1936.

———, ed. *État et santé, Cahiers de l'Institut allemand.* Paris: F. Sorlot, 1942.

Versnel, H. S. "Self-Sacrifice, Compensation, and the Anonymous God." In *Les sacrifices dans l'antiquité,* Entretiens Hardt, XXVII. Geneva: 1981.

Walton, Douglas N. *Brain Death: Ethical Considerations.* West Lafayette, Ind.: Purdue University Press, 1980.

Walzer, M. "The King's Trial and the Political Culture of Revolution." In *The French Revolution and the Creation of Modern Political Culture*, ed. Lucas Colin, vol. 2. Oxford: Pergamon, 1988.

Weinberg, Kurt. *Kafkas Dichtungen. Die Travestien des Mythos.* Bern: Francke, 1963.

Wilamowitz-Möllendorf, Ulrich von. *Platon.* Berlin: Weidmann, 1919.

Wilda, Wilhelm Eduard. *Das Strafrecht der Germanen.* Halle: C. A. Schwetschke, 1942.

Wundt, Wilhelm Max. *Völkerpsychologie.* Leipzig: W. Engelmann, 1905.

Index of Names

In this index an "f" after a number indicates a separate reference on the next page, and an "ff" indicates separate references on the next two pages. A continuous discussion over two or more pages is indicated by a span of page numbers, e.g., "57-59." *Passim* is used for a cluster of references in close but not consecutive sequence.

Crossing Aesthetics

Library of Congress Cataloging-in-Publication Data

Agamben, Giorgio
    [Homo sacer. English]
    Homo sacer : sovereign power and bare life / Giorgio Agamben.
        p.   cm. — (Meridian)
    Includes bibliographical references (p.   ) and index.
    ISBN 0-8047-3217-5 (cloth : alk. paper). — ISBN 0-8047-3218-3
    (paper : alk. paper)
        1. Human rights.   2. State, The.   3. Sovereignty.   4. Religion and
    politics.   5. Right to life.   6. Concentration camps.   I. Title.
    II. Series: Meridian (Stanford, Calif.)
    JC571.A16813   1998
    320'.01'1—dc21   97-36621

⊗ This book is printed on acid-free, recycled paper.

Original printing 1998

Last figure below indicates year of this printing:

16 15 14 13 12 11